DATE DUE

GAYLORD   PRINTED IN U.S.A.

JEFFERSON, NATIONALISM, AND THE ENLIGHTENMENT

Thomas Jefferson
A Philosopher a Patriote and a Friend
Dessiné par son Ami Tadée Kosciuszko.
Et Gravé par Mr. Sokolnicki.

JEFFERSON, NATIONALISM, AND THE ENLIGHTENMENT

—

Henry Steele Commager

*

George Braziller

NEW YORK

Frontispiece: A portrait of Jefferson drawn by Kosciuszko and engraved by Sokolnicki, The Metropolitan Museum of Art, The William H. Huntingdon Collection.

The lines quoted on page 109 are from Robert Frost's poem, "The Black Cottage," in *The Poetry of Robert Frost* edited by Edward Connery Lathem. Copyright 1930, 1939, © 1969 by Holt, Rinehart and Winston, Inc. Copyright © 1958 by Robert Frost. Copyright © 1967 by Lesley Frost Ballantine. Reprinted by permission of Holt, Rinehart and Winston, Inc.

Library of Congress Catalog Card Number: 74–80659
ISBN: 0–8076–1163–8

DESIGNED BY VINCENT TORRE
First paperback printing, September 1986
Printed in the United States of America

to

my old friend

Oskar Schotté

who

personifies the Enlightenment

ACKNOWLEDGMENTS

"America and the Enlightenment" was the opening lecture at the Library of Congress symposium on the American Revolution. It was published in *The Development of a Revolutionary Mentality*, Washington, 1972.

"The American Enlightenment and the Ancient World" was a contribution to the Festschrift für Karl Loewenstein aus Anlass Seines achtzigsten Geburtstages, Tübingen, 1971

"The Past as an Extension of the Present" was an address to the annual meeting of the American Antiquarian Society in 1969 and was printed in its Proceedings for that year.

"The Pursuit of Happiness" is reprinted from *Diogenes*, 1965 (offprint # 49)

"The Declaration of Independence" was written for *Thomas Jefferson: the Man and His World*, ed. by Lally Weymouth, N.Y. Putnam, 1972.

"Jefferson and the Enlightenment" appeared in abbreviated form in the same book.

"The Origins and Nature of American Nationalism" was first delivered as a lecture at the University of Liege in 1953. It was reprinted in abbreviated form in *The World of History*, ed. by Courtland Canby in 1954, and appears here in revised and expanded form.

CONTENTS

INTRODUCTION

A deceptive simplicity broods over the American Enlightenment: life, as pictured by a Crèvecoeur, a Chastellux, a Joel Barlow, a Timothy Dwight (all but Crèvecoeur left out slavery, so that simplified things a bit), politics, as illuminated in the writings of a Washington, a Jefferson, a Hamilton, a Tom Paine. Nor is this view of the Enlightenment as an era of simplicity, harmony, and virtue (how the eighteenth century rejoiced in "virtue") merely a phenomenon of hindsight—the view of Franklin's City of Brotherly Love through the smog of Mayor Rizzo's Philadelphia, the view of Monticello from San Clemente, the view of Valley Forge from My Lai. There was indeed a simplicity in the moral standards and in political faith—a simplicity reflected, as character is invariably reflected, in the language of the time: "we hold these truths to be self-evident"; "life, liberty, and the pursuit of happiness"; "government, like dress, is the badge of lost innocence"; "through all the gloom I can see the rays of ravishing light and glory. . . . Posterity will triumph in that day's transaction"; "to form a more pefect union"; "let us raise a standard to which the wise and the good can repair; the event is in the hands of God." What dignity and clarity and muscular vigor in the public address of a Hamilton, a Madison, a Jefferson, a Paine, a John Marshall; and what eloquence, too, when every word struck like a sword and every thought was like an arrow aflame. The contrast with public address today represents more than a change in style, it represents change in mind and morality: imagine General Westmoreland giving us a Circular Letter to the States like Washington's moving letter of 1783; imagine Mr. Nixon, who specializes in crises, writing Tom Paine's *Crisis* papers; imagine any three of our contemporary statesmen giving us *The Federalist Papers.*

"Politics is the divine science, after all," said John Adams, but it was not only in the realm of politics that the American *philosophes* displayed their sense of order, of harmany, of symmetry. These characterize the New England town, the architecture of Monticello, the music of Haydn and Mozart which Jefferson collected, the legal arguments of a Wilson and a Marshall, the passion for classification of flora and fauna, of languages, of races, indeed of all knowledge. Yet it was in the realm of politics that the American *philosophes* achieved their greatest triumphs.

Because the American *philosophes*, unlike their Old World counterparts, always appeared to be in control of the situation and able to master whatever problems arose (always excepting slavery of course), we are tempted to suppose that the problems themselves—compared to those which confront us today—were uncomplicated and lent themselves amiably to solution. That is an illusion, and a dangerous illusion, for it permits us to excuse our failures on the plausible argument that after all no other generation ever faced crises as grave as ours. The problems which confronted the Revolutionary generation were quite as complex, as importunate, and as frightening as those which confront us now. For a nation of some three millions (which meant a body politic of perhaps three-quarters of a million), divided into thirteen independent states, scattered over an immense territory without any system of roads or of communications, with no common organs of government, no common centers of economy, no common church, no common ruling class, and as yet no common loyalties—for such a nation to win independence, create a national government, invent the constitutional convention and write state and national constitutions which still endure, perfect a federal system, solve the ancient problem of colonialism, fix effective limits on government, separate church and state, establish genuine freedom of religion and of the press, impose order on a disorderly economy, deal with threats from Indians, the Spanish, and the British on every frontier, and develop the first working democracy, all in one generation, was without precedent in history and, we might add, without sequel too. The explanation of this outburst of constructive political genius is not to be found in the simplicity of the problems but in the sophistication, the sagacity, the creative intelligence of those who wrestled with them.

One thing that explains the logic and the harmony of their conduct, is that it reflected a deeper intellectual and moral harmony. They were, most of them, products of the Age of Reason —the phrase itself was coined by Thomas Paine. They lived in a universe which was controlled, in all its manifestations, by the laws of Nature and—if you will—of Nature's God. They knew that the same majestic laws which governed the movement of the stars in the heavens and of the tides in the oceans and the circulation of blood in the veins of man, governed too the great tides of human history, the rise and fall of empires, the operation of laws, and the functioning of the economy and the ultimate standards of morality. They knew that the laws which governed politics were ultimately the same as those which governed Nature herself, and they did not distinguish sharply between Natural Philosophy and Moral Philosophy. They had almost limitless confidence in Reason, in the ability of man to penetrate to the laws of Nature, to grasp their operations, and to apply them to the affairs of mankind. "It is comfortable," wrote Thomas Jefferson in 1786, "to see the standard of Reason at length erected, after so many ages during which the human mind has been held in vassalage by kings, priests and nobles, and it is honorable for us to have produced legislators who had the courage to declare that the Reason of man may be trusted with the formation of his own opinions." The Revolution was justified by an appeal to Reason, the constitutions were drawn up according to the principles of Reason, and to the *judiciary* was assigned greater authority than it had ever exercised before. In the whole of political literature is there a more reasonable document than *The Federalist Papers?* And along with Reason went History, for all knew that History was philosophy teaching by examples. The History they studied was simple enough—mostly the history of Greece and Rome, with a bit of French and English history thrown in for good measure. All very limited, by our standards, as their philosophy and their psychology was limited, but somehow it worked rather better than our modern explorations into psychology, into the formal analysis of public opinion, into the complexities of the histories of scores of nations work. They did not have the massive apparatus of the CIA and other intelligence gathering agencies to inform them of the dangers of a war in distant lands; they had, instead, Thucydides' account of the Sicilian expedition, and took that to heart: too bad Presidents Johnson and Nixon were not brought up on Thucydides! They did not need the contributions of psychoanalysis to enable them to understand the character of men they chose to high office; they fell back on Plutarch, who stood them in good stead, and ended up with Washington, Adams, Hamilton, Jefferson, Madison, Gallatin, Marshall, and their colleagues instead of with those who have guided our destinies during the past two decades.

All of this was common to the Western world, though each

nation had its special version of the Enlightenment. The young United States was part of that Western world, and the American Enlightenment was deeply indebted, philosophically, to the European. The American was an isolated society—more isolated geographically than is (let us say) New Zealand now, but it was cosmopolitan too: indeed it is probable that America was more cosmopolitan in the eighteenth century than at any time since. Even the Declaration of Independence was couched in cosmopolitan terms: it was a "decent respect to the opinions of mankind" that required a statement of causes, and the "facts" were submitted to a "candid world"—rather more than our government is prepared to do today even to its own people. The leaders of the American Enlightenment, too, were—for all their provincialism —cosmopolitan. They were deeply immersed in the literature of the ancient world and of the Old World; they were at home, many of them, in France and England—Jefferson surely, more at home in Paris than in Richmond, Franklin more at home in London than in Philadelphia. They thought of themselves as citizens of the world—Franklin who had his fingers in everything, Hamilton who would have been happy to live under George III, Jefferson who helped draw up the French Declaration of Rights, Tom Paine who was part of three revolutions, or two that succeeded and one that did not come off. They offered asylum to the victims of Old World tyranny—to Tom Paine and Priestley, to Van der Kemp and Mazzei, to Du Pont de Nemours and Benjamin Vaughan, and even to Tallyrand and Genet, and they conferred honorary citizenship on radicals who could not obtain a visa today. They were certain, too, that what they were engaged in was of momentous significance to all the peoples of the globe: Thus in a letter to the "Pennsylvania Farmer" John Dickinson, written only two days after he had become President, Jefferson confidently asserted that:

A just and solid republican government maintained here, will be a standing monument and example for the aim and imitation of the people of other countries [who] will see from our example that a free government is, of all others, the most energetic . . . that the inquiry which has been excited by our revolution and its consequences will ameliorate the condition of man over a great portion of the globe.

And fifteen years later he wrote exultantly to his old friend John Adams, who had long before slipped his Federalist moorings and was now afloat on Republican seas:

We are destined to be a barrier against the return of ignorance and barbarism. Old Europe will have to lean on our shoulders, and to hobble along by our side . . . as she can. What a colossus shall we be when the southern continent comes up to our mark! What a stand will it secure as a ralliance for the reason and freedom of the globe.

Probably no other generation in our history has been so conscious of its obligation to the rest of the human race—or at least to the European portion of it—or more ready to fulfill that mission which they fondly believed History had imposed upon them; no other took more completely for granted that the obligation and the mission were to be fulfilled by moral precept and practical example.

There was then a body of ideas and values common to the Enlightenment. Americans drew heavily on these ideas but contributed little to them: the American Enlightenment, after all, has nothing to show like the *Encyclopédie,* or Buffon's *Histoire Naturelle,* or the writings of a Voltaire—two hundred volumes of them—or of a Goethe; nothing to show like Winckelmann's study of Ancient Art, or David Hume's great *Inquiries,* or Immanuel Kant's *Critiques* or, for that matter, Thorwaldsen's marble statues or Mozart's *Così Fan Tutti.* True enough. But then the

Old World Enlightenment produced nothing like the constitutional convention, or the federal system, or Bills of Rights. The special quality of the American Enlightenment—it is a central theme of these essays—the quality which distinguished it most sharply from the European, is its constructive and consequential character; in this it foreshadowed that subsequent alliance of philosophy and conduct which has persuaded so many Europeans that America has no philosophy and deluded so many Americans into a belief that they do not need one.

For the American *philosophes* had jobs to do. They were not closet philosophers, perhaps they were not philosophers at all, they were working men. John Adams speculated and wrote, endlessly, about government, but he wrote the Constitution of Massachusetts, and was a pretty effective President; Jefferson wrote on everything from architecture to law, from religion to literature, from agriculture to morals, but he managed to write the Declaration of Independence, revise the laws of Virginia, draw up the Ordinances of 1784 and 1785, preside over the first real political party, and serve as President for two terms. He collected an immense library, but he also created the Library of Congress and provided it with a classification system. He made a pilgrimage to the Palladian palaces in the Veneto and sat gazing at the Temple in Nimes "like a lover gazing at his mistress," but he translated Palladio into the University of Virginia, and Nimes into the state capitol in Richmond. In America philosophers were not only kings, they were master craftsmen, not only dreamers but movers.

The prominence of Jefferson in these essays is not deliberate, neither is it fortuitous; it is, perhaps, inevitable, for though the American Enlightenment produced an extraordinary constellation of luminaries, of them all only Franklin can challenge the preeminence of Jefferson: and Franklin died at the birth of the Republic (1790) while Jefferson lived on for another thirty-six

xvii

years, active to the end. And though Jefferson occupied every important political post in the gift of his countrymen, his influence was as far-reaching in the philosophical, the cultural, the humanitarian as it was in the political arena. Of no one else in the American Enlightenment can it be said with such assurance that his talents were as affluent as his mind and his character and his style. He dominated the American stage more completely than Voltaire the French or Goethe the German or Joseph Banks —in a very different way—the English, or David Hume the Scottish. Jefferson has some claim to be considered the symbol of the Enlightenment everywhere, or at least of that late eighteenth-century Enlightenment which blended, almost imperceptibly, with Romanicism.

History should not be written with one eye cocked on the passing scene. These essays, written over a period of years, were not designed as current commentary; they attempted, rather, to recreate and if possible illuminate the American past in its own terms. But an introduction may be indulged in greater latitude than the essays themselves, for it is an amiable literary fiction that introductions are prefatory rather than conclusive. Here, then, I can ask more explicitly questions the essays themselves merely suggest.

No questions more importunate than these, as we study the birth of the American Republic: how did we get from Independence Hall to Watergate, from Yorktown to Vietnam, from Washington to Nixon? How did we get from Franklin's order to the American navy not to attack Captain Cook as he was engaged in work beneficial to mankind, to the vote in Congress banning the use of any American money for the relief of North Vietnamese children by the United Nations? How did we get from Tom Paine's proud boast: "But where is the King of America? ... Know that in America the law is King," to the official lawlessness of our own time? How did we get from Jefferson's great assertion of faith in his First Inaugural Address—"If there be any among us who would wish to destroy this union, or to change its republican form, let them stand undisturbed as monuments of the safety with which error of opinion can be tolerated where reason is left free to combat it,"— to the use of surveillance, wiretapping, security checks, censorship, and *agents provocateurs?* How did we get from *The Federalist Papers* to the White House Transcripts? And how did we get from an unquestioning acceptance of the axiom that eternal vigilance is the price of liberty to the kind of petulant boredom we display towards revelations of duplicity, mendacity, corruption, and turpitude without parallel in our history?

We could go on and on, but the contrast is sufficiently obvious. It is obvious, too, if we turn from the particular to the general, what happened to that deep sense of obligation to the past that animated most of the Founding Fathers, the obligation to preserve the heritage of civilization from Judea and Greece and Rome and, in the political and constitutional arena, from the Mother Country—a commitment which linked the new nation, even as she was embarking upon the boldest of experiments, irrevocably to the Old World, so that the most innovative of revolutions was also the most conservative? What happened to the deep and passionate sense of fiduciary obligation to posterity which animated all the Founding Fathers and admonished them to pass on their heritage intact to their descendants, even "to the thousandth and thousandth generation"? What happened to that devotion to the commonwealth which animated a Franklin, an Adams, a Jefferson, a Washington, a Mason, a Madison, a Wilson to wear out their lives, and their fortunes too, in the public service, and which gave us, in a single generation, a galaxy of public leaders we have never been able remotely to duplicate since then? What happened to that ingenuity, that resourcefulness, that creativity which fashioned, again in a single generation, all those great political institutions on whose capital we have been living ever since? What happened to that confidence in Reason, and in the ability of men to solve their most formidable problems by the application of Reason; to that confidence in the ultimate common sense and even wisdom of the people—a confidence which was at the basis of the passion for freedom of the human mind in every area, religion, politics, science, and morals?

When we have answered these questions we may perhaps set about restoring the intellectual and moral world which the Enlightenment created, and which we have lost or betrayed. That is the most important item on the agenda of the Bicentennial years.

HENRY STEELE COMMAGER

Amherst, Mass.

JEFFERSON,
NATIONALISM,
AND THE
ENLIGHTENMENT

1

---

*AMERICA
AND THE
ENLIGHTENMENT*

Mᴀ ᴛʜᴇᴍᴇ can be put simply and succinctly, though I am aware that simplicity is deceptive and succinctness suspect. It is this: that the Old World imagined the Enlightenment and the New World realized it. The Old World invented it, formulated it, and agitated it; America absorbed it, reflected it, and institutionalized it.

Intellectually eighteenth-century America was very much part of the European Enlightenment—particularly in its English, Scottish, and French manifestations; indeed, philosophically Europe and America may have been more nearly one world in that era than in any since. Almost everywhere the *philosophes* embraced a common body of ideas, subscribed to a common body of laws, shared a common faith. They were all natural philosophers—what we call scientists—and if they were not all trained in science, they were fascinated by it and dabbled in it: Voltaire, who early provided a simplified Newton; Goethe, who wrote learnedly (if mistakenly) on optics; Priestley, who invented not only Unitarianism but oxygen and soda water and wrote a history of electricity; Struensee, who was after all a medical doctor; Lord Monboddo, who anticipated organic evolution; and in

3

America the members of the Philosophical Society—Franklin, Jefferson, Rittenhouse, Dr. Rush—and elsewhere a Manasseh Cutler, who combined botanizing with empire building, a Hugh Williamson, who was both doctor and ethnologist as well as historian, a Benjamin Thompson of Woburn, Mass., who became Count Rumford of the Holy Roman Empire and founded the Royal Institution in London and endowed the Rumford Chair of Natural Sciences at Harvard College.

They accepted the Newtonian world governed by laws of Nature and (if you wished to make gestures, as did Jefferson and Voltaire, or more than gestures, as did Newton himself) of Nature's God. They accepted, too, the principle of the sovereignty of Reason, and the axiom that Reason could penetrate to and master the laws of Nature and of God, and that it could persuade men to conform to them, not only in philosophy and ethics, but in politics, economy, law, education, even in art and literature, for they knew that:

> All are but parts of one stupendous Whole
> Whose body Nature is, and God the soul.

And they accepted—even those who like Albrecht von Haller had no use for its author—Voltaire's dictum that "God has given us a principle of universal Reason as He has given feathers to birds and fur to bears." It was Reason that guided the legal thinking of Blackstone and of his greatest critic, Bentham; Reason that reorganized the national economy in Austria and Prussia along cameralist lines; Reason that provided the arguments for the Declaration of Independence; and the great Jacques-Louis David announced that "the genius of the arts needs no other guide than the torch of Reason." Looking back over half a century, Jefferson celebrated the animating principle of his age:

4

We believed that man was a rational animal. . . . We believed that men, habituated to thinking for themselves, and to follow their reason as guide, would be more easily and safely governed than with minds nourished in error and vitiated and debased by ignorance.

Faith in Nature and in Reason was one of the common denominators of the Enlightened Despots too (an absurd term, that, but we seem to be stuck with it), and of the *philosophes* they sometimes attracted or seduced to their courts: of Frederick in Prussia, Leopold in Tuscany, Joseph in Austria, Catherine in Russia, Gustavus III in Sweden, or Charles in Baden; of Pombal in Portugal, Campomanes in Spain, Struensee in Denmark, Tanucci in Naples, Goethe in Weimar, even, off and on, Turgot or Necker in France; and certainly of American *philosophes* like Franklin, Jefferson, John Adams, and Tom Paine.

From Newtonian premises there followed, logically, a passion for order that regulated almost every form of expression. "Order," their most representative poet had told them, "is Heav'n's First Law," and they made it theirs (at least when not too inconvenient), for they yearned to be in harmony with the will of Heaven. How they organize, how they codify, how they systematize and classify, and all Nature falls into order at their bidding! Thus Linnaeus imposed a *System of Nature* on all flora and fauna and Buffon on almost everything else, in his prodigious *Histoire Naturelle*; thus the *Encyclopédistes*, not content with organizing knowledge in the greatest of literary enterprises, ultimately reorganized it all in the *Encyclopédie Méthodique* (eventually in 201 volumes). René Réaumur devoted six volumes to classification of insects; Albrecht von Haller gave five volumes to *Flora Helvitica* and eight to human anatomy: and the Baron d'Holbach organized everything into an ambitious *Système de la Nature*. Bentham tried to codify the laws of England; Americans for the first time

5

systematized not only laws but rights in their constitutions; the Comte Real de Curban analyzed the science of government in eight volumes, and Filangieri created a science of legislation in six, and the Duc de Luynes devoted a lifetime to drawing up an orderly social register for the French aristocracy in seventeen volumes. Order, too, presided over the chamber music of Mozart and Haydn, the gardens at Versailles and Schönbruun, the palaces and country houses of Eigtved in Copenhagen and Robert Adam in Edinburgh and Jacques Gabriel in Paris; order controlled the brush of Canaletto and the chisel in the hands of Thorwaldsen.

A third common denominator of the Enlightenment was both a prerequisite and a product of the first: commitment to freedom of the mind—freedom from religious and social superstitions, freedom from the tyranny of the Church, the state, and the academy, freedom to follow the teachings of science and of reason wherever they led. From this followed inevitably war upon those institutions that threatened freedom; *écrasez l'infâme* was, symbolically at least, the rallying cry of the Old World Enlightenment, though not of the New, for the New had no *infâme* to crush. Jefferson's affirmation was even more appropriate than Voltaire's *cri de coeur:* "I have sworn upon the altar of God, eternal hostility against every form of tyranny over the mind of man." Outside America, few would dare take in quite that much territory.

They knew what to do with their free minds, too. Even more than the men of the Renaissance they were launched on voyages of discovery of new worlds, new ideas, new peoples, new societies, new civilizations, new laws; new flora and fauna, new and brighter stars in the skies and new and darker recesses of the human mind, new aspects of nature and of human nature, all their most representative figures participated in this great enterprise. They sailed with Captain Cook and Joseph Banks (that

6

great entrepreneur of ideas who was to head the Royal Society for forty-two years) to chart the transit of Venus and find new continents, or they walked with the Connecticut Yankee John Ledyard from Paris to Yakutsk to ascertain the common ties that bound Asia and Alaska; they gazed at the heavens with Herschel, who doubled the known universe, or experimented with Priestley and Lavoisier in their chemical laboratories; with Winckelmann and Niebuhr they uncovered ancient civilization and with Colden and Bartram and Jefferson himself they studied the American Indian. With Montesquieu and Gibbon they explored the causes of the rise and decline of empires and with Christian Wolff and Voltaire and William Chambers they penetrated to the mind and the art of China; with Rousseau and Pestalozzi they opened up a new world of childhood, and with the fantastic Lord Monboddo they promoted the orangutan to his rightful place in the chain of being.

The *philosophes* shared a fourth passion and commitment: a humanitarianism which imagined and fought for the abolition of torture and the amelioration of the barbarous penal code that still disgraced the statute books of even the most civilized nations; an end to the Inquisition; improvement in the lot of the peasants and the serfs; the abolition of the slave trade and even of slavery itself —all that might contribute to the enhancement of private and public happiness. It is here that the Enlightenment blended almost imperceptibly into Romanticism, for what more romantic notion than that society had an obligation to advance the happiness of its people.

Their ultimate objective was, of course, to liberate the minds and the energies of men to achieve what Providence had so clearly intended: to conform so perfectly to the laws of Nature that the errors, evils, and corruptions which had for so long afflicted mankind would vanish and man would enter a new golden age. An exhilarating program this, but the agenda of the

7

old world *philosophes* was not exhilarating; it was almost wholly negative. For the *philosophes* were helpless against the weaponry of the state, the Church, the Inquisition, the law, the military, even the universities, which bristled on every quarter of the horizon. These could not, in fact, be overthrown; they had to be circumvented, placated, or won over, and in most countries the energies of the *philosophes* were devoted to the elementary task of survival: Diderot cast into jail, and the *Encyclopédie* banned; Voltaire in hiding or in exile; Rousseau on the run; Tom Paine outlawed; Pietro Gianonne languishing in jail in Turin for the audacities of his *History of Naples;* even the great Buffon forced to retract all those portions of his *Histoire Naturelle* to which the Church objected. Before the *philosophes* could begin the great task of reconstruction there had to be a clearing away of censorship, the Inquisition, torture, corruption, arbitrary power—of a hundred evils, each one, it seemed, hydra-headed.

And how was this to be achieved? Not through suffrage, for except in England and Holland and some of the Swiss cantons there was no suffrage to speak of, and not much even in these more liberal countries. Not by an appeal to public opinion, for even if here and there an elitist opinion existed, there was really no way in which it could be made politically effective. Not by working through the Church or the universities, for these were an essential part of the establishment, and outside Scotland and Holland and a few of the German states the universities were moribund. No, the great enterprise of liberation and freedom, if it was to succeed, must be adopted by princes and monarchs who were themselves *philosophes.*

*

All the philosophers, European and American alike, were trained on the classics, and all knew Plato's prediction that there would

8

be "no end to the troubles of states, or indeed, of humanity itself until philosophers became kings in this world, or until those we now call kings and rulers, really and truly become philosophers." There were no philosophers who were kings, though Goethe may have imagined himself one, but all the kings were philosophers, or pretended to be, and if they were not they hastened to attach philosophers to their courts so they could be respectable. Consider Frederick of Prussia: did not Voltaire and Diderot and La Grange and Maupertuis all testify that he was a philosopher, the very paragon of philosophers? Or consider the Empress Catherine, the Semiramis of the North, who combined the wisdom of Solon and the justice of Lycurgus (so said Diderot, who ought to know; so said the Baron Grimm, who gave her all the literary gossip for twenty-two years). She invited Voltaire to her court, in vain. She invited d'Alembert to tutor her grandson, and when he refused to come she imported Frédéric de La Harpe, the young man who had won a prize for the best address on *Peace*— just what most interested Catherine! She invited Beccaria from Milan to reform her penal code, but nothing happened; she even invited Diderot to draw up a model educational plan, which he did and which she promptly forgot. And up in frozen Stockholm was the brilliant young Gustavus III. He had seized the reins of power, he had knocked Hats and Caps off hard Swedish heads, he had established freedom of the press and ended torture, he founded the Swedish Academy, he patronized poets, he adored the opera, and the muses rewarded him with immortality by turning his murder at a masked ball into just such an opera as would have delighted him. There was Karl Friedrich of Baden who wrote a book on physiocracy and was so enlightened that he determined "to make his subjects into free, opulent and law-abiding citizens whether they liked it or not," and there was Karl August who ruled Weimar and made that tiny duchy a showplace of Europe, what with Goethe and Schiller and

9

Wieland, to say nothing of Herder and Fichte.

And where the kings were not sufficiently enlightened their ministers were: the mighty Pombal, who rebuilt Portugal after the Lisbon earthquake, and the incomparable Sonnenfels in Vienna, the son of a rabbi—think how enlightened that was of Maria Theresa—and, for a time Campomanes in Spain, and Struensee in Denmark, who turned everything upside down in fourteen months, and in Munich Count Rumford, who introduced not only order but potato soup into Bavaria. It was all a mutual admiration society, too. The kings indulged the *philosophes*, and the *philosophes* extolled the kings: all worked together for the happiness of man.

It is all too good to be true. Alas, it is not true. The play is so brilliant, the lines are so witty, the plot is so intricate, the setting so polished, the costumes so splendid, the music so enchanting, that we sit enthralled through it all. Then the last lines are spoken and the actors depart, and the lovely tunes are only an echo lingering on in our mind, and the whole thing is a dream. We look at the stage and it is no longer a stage: it is no longer the Seville of the Barber, but of the Inquisition; no longer the London of the *Beggar's Opera*, but of Gin Alley; no longer the Naples of *Così Fan Tutte*, but of Ferdinand IV crushing the revolution and the romantic Prince Caracciolo hanging from the yardarm of Lord Nelson's *Minerva*; no longer the Venice of Goldoni, but of Giorgine Pisani who had appealed to the populace against the inquisitors and was allowed to rot in jail. Catherine no longer plays the role of the Semiramis of the North, and when the wretched Alexander Radischev wrote a book depicting the hard lot of the serfs she shipped him off to Siberia; worse yet, she relegated all her busts of Voltaire and Diderot to the basement! In Copenhagen Struensee was drawn and quartered for violating the queen and the privileges of the nobility; and over in Norway a leader of the peasants, Christian Lofthuus, deluded himself that he had a mandate from the king to speak for his countrymen: he was chained to a block of stone in the fortress of Christiania and left to rot.

Now what everybody does—così fan tutte—is no longer to play at love and war. No, the bugles that sound are real bugles and the drumbeats will soon roll across the whole of Europe. The armies march and Poland is dismembered. Now Goldoni is dead and the Venetian Republic is no more, and Wordsworth can write those elegiac lines. In faraway Quito the patriot Dr. Espejo is tortured to death for reprinting the Declaration of the Rights of Man, and in Portuguese Bahia four radicals who called for equality in a democratic republic are hanged. Now the comedy is over and reality takes charge. That is why it is not Giovanni descending into Hell while all the happy swains and maids stand singing in the courtyard, or Floristan rescued from the dungeon, or Casanova with still another conquest; in the end it is "infuriated man, seeking through blood and slaughter his long lost liberty," seeking it but not finding it. In the end the philosophers were not kings, nor even next to kings: Turgot dismissed, Necker dismissed, Count Rumford expelled, the mighty Pombal disgraced, Johann Moser languishing in solitary confinement, Struensee beheaded, Brissot guillotined, Condorcet dead in that jail in Bourg-la-Reine, a copy of Horace in his pocket. The few who retained power—Sonnenfels in Austria, Tanucci in Naples, Pitt in London, for example, conveniently forgot most of their liberal principles for, like their masters, they were frightened out of their wits by the spectacle of liberalism translated from philosophy to politics.

All true enough, but not in America. The waves of reaction lapped at that distant shore but did not inundate it. It was Jefferson who was elected President in 1800, not Aaron Burr or Fisher Ames.

II

*

Americans had no kings, not after they had toppled George III anyway. No kings, no aristocracy, no church in the Old World sense of the term, no bishops, no inquisition, no army, no navy, no colonies, no peasantry, no proletariat. But they had philosophers in plenty. Every town had its Solon, its Cato, and certainly —as John Trumbull made clear in *M'Fingal*—its Honorius. And if the philosophers were not kings they were something better— they were the elected representatives of the sovereign people. In America, and in America alone, the people had deliberately chosen to be ruled by philosophers: Washington, Adams, Jefferson, Madison in the presidential chair; a Bowdoin, a Jay, a Jonathan Trumbull, a Franklin, a Clinton, a Pinckney, a Livingston in the gubernatorial—and you can go on and on. Now that we are busy celebrating the traditions of the Revolutionary era, this is one tradition we would do well to revive—philosophers as kings.

Not many of them, to be sure, could devote all their energies to statecraft or philosophy, for they were more like Cincinnatus than like Caesar, busy with farming or the law, and in any event they lacked the courts, the churches, the academies, the universities, which provided so much of the patronage, the nurture, and the security for *philosophes* in the Old World. Yet politics and "universal reformation" were not an avocation with them, a game, as one so often senses they were in the Old World. They were a serious matter, a lifelong consecration—just what Jefferson meant when he wrote, for the Congress, that "we mutually pledge to each other our lives, our fortunes and our sacred honor"; just what Washington meant in his eloquent circular letter to the states of 1783:

The foundation of our empire was not laid in the gloomy age of ignorance and superstition, but at an epocha when the rights of mankind were better understood and more clearly defined, than at any former period, the researches of the human mind after social happiness have been carried to a greater extent, the treasures of knowledge . . . are laid open for our use, and their collected wisdom may be happily applied in the establishment of our forms of government.

In America, and perhaps alone in America, statesmen and philosophers were not required to curry favor with capricious monarchs or to bend the knee to power (I am not forgetting the counterargument of a capricious electorate), nor were they required to exhaust their energies in sweeping away the anachronisms which littered the landscape of history. Here they were able to translate their ideas into institutions. This is a major difference between the New and the Old World Enlightenments —that in America the people, not the enlightened monarchs or professional philosophers, were able to get on with the job, and did.

No need, here, to war against feudalism because, except for vestigial remains like primogeniture and entail, which fell almost without a struggle, there was none. No need to topple a ruling class (the exodus of the loyalists had simplified matters here, no doubt), for by Old World standards there was no ruling class, certainly none that was legally entitled to rule or to enjoy special privileges, unless you regard the whole of the white population as in that category. Neither wealth, nor education, nor family could confer privilege in national affairs, only color: under the Constitution adopted in 1788 any free white man could hold the office of President, Justice of the Supreme Court, Secretary of State, or minister, no matter how rich or poor, how devout or agnostic, how learned or ignorant. No need to struggle against the power and pretensions of the military, or the threat of a "standing army"—which was almost an obsession. After the treaty of peace the army stood at 840 men and 46 officers; when Washington took office it was increased to 1,216 men and 57 officers! No need, either, to throw the army open to talent. In France at that time the officer corps consisted of 6,353 nobles and 1,845 commoners and "soldiers of fortune," and in Prussia a few years later there were 700 commoners in an officer corps of 7,100. No wonder a French officer in the American army reported with incredulity that "our inn-keeper was a captain, and there are shoemakers who are colonels"; no wonder Cassius (he was really Aedanus Burke but Cassius sounded more appropriate) assailed the innocuous Society of the Cincinnati as if it were to be a new hereditary nobility that would surely subvert the liberties of America!

No need to struggle against the censorship which everywhere, except perhaps in Holland, hovered like a black cloud over the enterprises of the *philosophes*—the *Encyclopédie*, for example—and which hurried so many of them into flight: Rousseau to England, Raynal to Holland, Voltaire to Geneva (where they publicly burned his *Philosophical Dictionary*), Priestley to Pennsylvania, Van der Kemp to New York, Madame de Staël to Coppet. No need to repudiate a censorship which condemned the wretched Abbé Dubourg to a lingering death in an iron cage for a harmless squib called *The Chinese Spy* and sentenced to life imprisonment a poor woman who had been caught peddling a copy of Holbach's *Christianity Unmasked;* which in Württemberg jailed the great scholar-statesman Johann Moser (he wrote 266 books) for five years for criticizing the financial irresponsibility of Karl Eugen; which outlawed Tom Paine for the crime of *The Rights of Man* (it went through twenty-one editions in the United States without doing any perceptible harm); which, after 1789, banned all French books from Russia; and which denied Immanuel Kant the right

to publish or lecture on religion. No need for all this, for there
was no censorship, or none that mattered. No need to agitate for
the end of torture—an end to the spectacle of Calas broken on the
wheel or La Barré tortured and burned or a wretched Milanese
youth tortured and executed for shouting, in a church, "Long
live liberty"—for torture was unknown to American law.

No need to campaign for the secularization of education. It
was, by Old World standards, already secularized. One of the
purposes of creating public schools in the Bay Colony was to
outwit "ye ould deluder Satan," but that maneuver was directed
by the secular branch of the community, not the ecclesiastical, or
—if it was difficult to make this distinction in the 1640s—that was
certainly true during the era of the Enlightenment. No religious
tests sifted applicants to colleges and universities (not until 1871
could dissenters attend the universities of Oxford or Cambridge),
nor were there religious tests for professors. In the seventeenth
century a Baptist sat in the president's chair at Harvard College,
and in the opening days of the nineteenth century a Unitarian
was elected to the Hollis Chair of Divinity (As late as 1862, Cambridge University turned down a professorship of American history on the ground that the incumbent might be a Unitarian!).
The charter of the College of Rhode Island, established especially
for the proper training of Baptists, provided that "all members
shall forever enjoy free, absolute, and uninterrupted liberty of
conscience" and that the board of trustees should include Angli-
cans, Congregationalists, and Quakers. So, too, trustees of the
new College of Philadelphia included Presbyterians and Angli-
cans, as well as Quakers, and Franklin, who was a deist, served
as the first president of the board. Jefferson's new University of
Virginia was based on "the illimitable freedom of the human
mind." "Here," he wrote, "we are not afraid to follow truth
wherever it may lead, nor to tolerate any error as long as reason
is left free to combat it." And, needless to say, where the state

universities of the Old World faithfully reflected the established religion, the new American state universities which emerged, on paper at least, in the 1780s, embraced as a matter of course the principle of religious freedom for students and faculty alike.

Everywhere in the Old World the Church shared with the crown responsibility for the minds and souls of the people, and we know from the heated debates on the modification of the Test Acts throughout much of the eighteenth century how sacred this connection was assumed to be, and how pernicious any slightest rent in the seamless web of conformity. Rich, formidable, and intractable, the Church controlled almost everything it touched, and there was not much that it did not touch. It guarded the gates of universities and would not permit dissenters to enter; it censored literature and scholarship and science, too: the Sorbonne rejected the doctrines of William Harvey and Salamanca those of Newton, and in Denmark the Church fought some of the medical reforms of Dr. Struensee—even when he was prime minister—on the ground that they were sacrilegious. It sat on the benches of the courts, dispensed justice and injustice, and hanged Pastor Rochette for conducting Protestant services, and the Anglican Establishment would no more tolerate Catholic teachers than Catholic priests in Ireland. The Church owned half the soil of Tuscany, Portugal, and Belgium and exercised political as well as ecclesiastical jurisdiction over vast areas of Italy and Spain. And it exiled 18,000 Protestants from the archbishopric of Salzburg, 1,200 of whom eventually found refuge in Georgia.

Nowhere in the American colonies or states was there an established church that enjoyed power even remotely comparable to that enjoyed by establishments almost everywhere in Europe. What Crèvecoeur observed in the third of his letters was generally true, that persecution, religious pride, contradiction, are the food of what the world commonly calls religion. These motives have ceased here. Zeal in Europe is confined; here it evaporates in the great distance it has to travel. There it is a grain of powder enclosed; here it burns away in the open air and consumes without effect.

An Isaac Backus might protest this genial view of the American religious scene. The interesting thing—interesting assuredly to Old World observers—is that he did, and that in his famous confrontation with John Adams on religious liberty, it was Adams who was embarrassed, and that in the end the greatest champion of religious liberty in New England since Roger Williams was able to accept the religious provisions (or nonprovisions) of both the Massachusetts and the United States Constitutions.

Consider the familiar, even hackneyed, story of the struggle for religious freedom in Virginia. There the Anglican establishment was as powerful, as rich, and as socially distinguished as anywhere else in the United States—or so it seemed. In 1776, however, Mason's Bill of Rights established religious freedom in the new state, and in 1779 the church was quietly disestablished, almost without a furor. That same year Jefferson (himself a formal though not precisely a devout Anglican) prepared a bill to separate church and state. Patrick Henry attempted to circumvent the proposal by the clever stratagem of providing aid for all denominations, and the struggle was on. With his famous "Remonstrance" Madison rallied support to the principle of complete separation, and in 1785 and 1786 Jefferson's statute of religious liberty was triumphantly enacted. Jefferson described the campaign for separation of church and state as "the severest contest in which I have ever been engaged." If that were indeed true, it would cast a roseate glow on the American scene. For no one in Virginia—or elsewhere in America—went to the stake for his faith (the Reverend Jonathan Boucher was burned in effigy, but not for his religious views!); none was forced to flee to a more hospitable climate, none was ousted from his pulpit or his university, none was subject to censorship or even to contumely. We cannot but wonder what Voltaire would have thought of Jefferson's observation, or any one of the scores of *philosophes* who wore out their lives, and sometimes lost them, in a vain struggle to overthrow the *infâme*.

*

The institutionalization of Enlightenment principles was political and constitutional. We take that for granted but the Old World could not: statesmen there had to content themselves with Pope's admonition:

> For forms of government let fools contest,
> What e'er is best administered is best.

They made important contributions to administrative reform, but few to politics and none to constitutionalism. The constitutions which glimmer fitfully in the literature of the day are daydreams of the *philosophes*: Rousseau's model constitutions for Corsica and Poland, for example, or the blanket *Code de la Nature* of Morelly (the poor fellow has no other name, and perhaps no existence), or the Abbé Mably's constitution for Poland and for American states too—he even claimed credit for the constitution of Massachusetts—or G. E. Lamprecht's curious design for an ideal government for Prussia which assigned to the monarch responsibility for "making the citizens in every regard more well behaved, healthier, wiser, richer and more secure," or von Haller's *Usong* with its wonderful summary of the duties of an enlightened despot. When it came to making real constitutions, however, Europe had little to show. The French tried a dozen, which did not work; the Americans made do with one, which did.

There is a paradox here, one to which we are so accustomed that we scarcely appreciate it. Surely anyone looking objectively at the world of the eighteenth century might have concluded that although Americans had a certain shrewdness about local government, they did not have true political sophistication, not the kind of political talent needed for solving those intractable problems which for more than two millennia had been glaring upon mankind. Such talent, surely, was to be found in the busy haunts of men—the courts, the capitals, the great universities and academies—of the Old World, not in some pastoral paradise such as Crèvecoeur had imagined. But that is not the way it turned out. It was, in the end, Americans who proved sophisticated. How fascinating that the people most deeply committed to the principle of the supremacy of law over man should be perhaps the only one where the principle was not really needed, and that the people most profoundly suspicious of power in government should be perhaps the only one whose leaders seemed immune to the corruptions of power.

How paradoxical, too, that from a society of three million, with a body politic of perhaps half a million, spread thin over an immense territory, with no populous cities, no great centers of learning, and no tradition of high politics, should come in one generation the most distinguished galaxy of statesmen to be found anywhere in that century or, perhaps, since. You will remember that Jefferson made precisely this point in *Notes on the State of Virginia*, where he asserts with the straightest of faces that on the basis of population France should have eight Washingtons and eight Franklins. (Was it modesty that kept him from adding eight Jeffersons, too, or the realization that this would occur to all his readers?) And how astonishing, too—indeed so providential that perhaps only a Parson Weems could do it justice—that the generation which presided over the birth of the Republic stayed on to direct its destinies for another fifty years!

"Politics is the divine science, after all," wrote John Adams, who somehow never mastered it, and the author of *Notes on Virginia*, though he shunned the term divine, nevertheless agreed that

> the creation of a proper political system was the whole object of the revolution, for should a bad government be instituted for us in the future, it would have been as well to have accepted at first the bad one offered to us from beyond the water.

"Creation" is perhaps the most interesting word here—for if American political principles were not new, the mechanisms were. What impresses us—particularly now in our current phase of intellectual impotence and political sterility—is precisely the resourcefulness, the fecundity, the creative energy of that generation. As Tom Paine observed in *The Rights of Man*,

> the case and circumstances of America present themselves as in the beginning of a world. . . . We have no occasion to roam for information into the obscure fields of antiquity, nor hazard ourselves upon conjecture. We are brought at once to the point of seeing government begin, as if we had lived in the beginning of time.

What the Americans of the Revolutionary generation did is too familiar to justify rehearsal. What they did was to put on the road to solution almost all those great problems which had bemused and perplexed political thinkers from ancient times. They turned to the enduring problem of the origin and authority of government, and announced that government derived its just powers from the consent of the governed, who had the right, when they wished, to institute new governments. And they proceeded to

institutionalize that great principle in the constitutional convention—it was almost the private invention of John Adams. They
turned to the even more difficult problem of placing limits on
power and undertook to solve it by a complex network of institutions and mechanisms: the written constitution as a body of
"supreme law"; bills of rights which for the first time guaranteed
substantive as well as procedural rights; separation of powers—
separation rather than the British "balance"—and an elaborate
scheme of internal checks and balances, including that of nation
and state; and—after some experimentation—judicial review.
They took the idea of federalism, which had never worked successfully, solved its most complex problem of the distribution of
powers, and its most importunate problem of sanctions, and
created the first successful and enduring federal government.
The British Empire had been wrecked on the rocks of colonialism. Americans, with their independence, inherited colonies as
large as the original thirteen states; they disposed of their colonial
problem by the simple device—which no one had thought of
since the days of the Greek city-states—of doing away with colonies altogether and calling them states. They contrived instruments and devices for making these institutions work: an incomparably broader suffrage than obtained anywhere else in the
western world, and a broader participation in community affairs,
too, than in any other communities except possibly Iceland and
some of the smaller Swiss cantons. Add atop this an elected chief
executive, a really independent judiciary—something no European state could boast—and, perhaps most original of all, political parties much more responsive and effective than the Hats and
Caps of Sweden or the Whigs and Tories, the factions and cliques
of British politics.

Nor should we forget those other remarkable innovations, or
creations, quite as important in their way as the political or
constitutional: the establishment of true freedom of the press; the

achievement of a broader literacy than was to be found elsewhere in the western world, and with it provision for public education which reached a larger proportion of the population than it did elsewhere; and finally a growth of social and economic equality beyond anything to be found in the Old World.

This achievement dramatizes the most tragic failure of the American Enlightenment: the failure to put Negro slavery on the road to extinction. The failure was not—I know there are some who will disagree with this—a failure of the American Enlightenment but rather a failure of Romanticism. But that is another story.

The frustration of the bright hopes of a Jefferson, a Rush, a Benezet, a Jay, and so many others, does in turn dramatize one striking feature of the American Enlightenment which again is taken for granted or misinterpreted: that it did not collapse into revolution or reaction. There was no American Thermidor, not even in the philosophical and intellectual arena. Loyalists who might have led such a reaction either had left or had returned reconciled; the hard times of the confederation period did not lead to disillusionment with the achievements of the war, or to a repudiation of the great advances in politics, humanitarianism, and reform. At a time when the French were turning to Napoleon the Americans turned to Jefferson, and the Jeffersonian era outlasted the Napoleonic.

The passion and the zeal for institutionalization extended to the realm of moral philosophy: even in America it was not just romantics like Jefferson and Tom Paine and Joel Barlow who invoked it, but stout realists like John Adams and George Washington.

John Adams, who rarely agreed with anyone, wrote in 1776 that "upon this point all speculative politicians will agree, that the happiness of society is the end of government, as all divines and moral philosophers will agree that the happiness of the individual is the end of man." Washington referred to happiness or felicity five times in the central paragraph of his Circular to the States of 1783, and Crèvecoeur no less than thirteen times in the second of his *Letters.* The Virginia Bill of Rights guaranteed the right not only to pursue but to obtain happiness. Jefferson did not go quite that far, but he went to immortality. It was a theme he returned to again and again—remember that lovely line in the first inaugural which invokes the blessings of "Providence, which by all its dispensations proves that it delights in the happiness of man here, and his greater happiness hereafter." I like best his letter to Maria Cosway, over in France, with whom he conducted what by modern standards was a very low-key flirtation, congratulating her on the birth of a daughter. "They tell me *que vouz allez faire un enfant. . . .* You may make children there, but this is the country to transplant them to. There is no comparison between the sum of happiness enjoyed there and here."

*

Two other large philosophical concepts of the Enlightenment—preoccupations even—lent themselves only grudgingly to institutionalization in the Old World, but vindicated such institutionalization in the New. One was deeply rooted in European thought, the other was largely a product of American experience. I refer to the doctrine of progress and to the philosophy of history as prospective rather than retrospective.

Consider first the idea of progress, that *ignis fatuus* which glimmered before the fascinated gaze of so many of the *philosophes* of the Old World and which was so speedily and so tragically juxtaposed with its own repudiation, as it were, in the drama of a Condorcet clutching the *Equisse* (metaphorically at least) as he took his own life, and of the confrontation, just two months later, between Coffinhal and Lavoisier: "The Republic has no need of *savants"* (if it is not literally true, it is *ben trováto*). How the *philosophes* rejoiced in the discomfiture of the ancients by the moderns, in the spread of the empire of reason, in the reinforcements from China, in the ability of Diderot to overcome every obstacle and bring the *Encyclopédie* to a triumphant conclusion, in the expulsion of the Jesuits, in the growth of prosperity and, above all, of population, that most visible, that most irrefutable, argument for progress.

Americans, too, embraced the doctrine of progress, but they produced no analytical treatises, no formal programs, no utopian models. That is not because they were not conscious of progress, but because they took it for granted. Well might they affirm that all their reports on America were studies in progress, all their political programs manifestations of progress, all their statistics demonstrations of progress, and that as for utopian romances, what was America herself but a utopian romance? The formal literature which Americans produced on progress is negligible, but the idea of progress suffuses much of the writing of the day, and shines forth with special radiance from the writings of Franklin, Jefferson, Tom Paine, Joel Barlow, Dr. Rush, even from the writings of stout conservatives like Ezra Stiles and Timothy Dwight.

How different the notion of progress in the Old World and the New! It was, we are tempted to say, a different concept masquerading under the same name. The ultimate goal is doubtless the same on both sides of the Atlantic (though even that can be questioned)—the triumph of reason and the achievement of happiness—but the meaning of these terms received very different readings.

In the Old World (these generalizations are of course wholly lacking in cautious discrimination) progress meant chiefly improvement in the arts, learning, and science, and the gradual refinement of manners and perhaps even of morals. Thus at the very beginning of the great inquiry, d'Alembert's *Preliminary Discourse* to the *Encyclopédie* refers to "progress of the mind," "philosophy," "erudition and belles lettres," "the attitude toward human knowledge," and so forth. And here, forty years later, is Dodson's edition of the *Encyclopaedia*—which, unlike the *Encyclopédie*, was published in America—somehow equating civilization with "magnificent buildings, noble statues, paintings expressive of life and passion, and poems." No suggestion here (though the article appeared under the rubric "Society") that the well-being of the masses, the amelioration of slavery or of the penal code, or the reign of peace were involved in progress, and no wonder, for in the end the author embraces the cyclical theory of history and thus disposes of progress altogether.

Progress, in the Old World, was a class concept, too, something the *philosophes* could formulate and the nobility and the intellectuals enjoy. Even the most ardent critics of the establishment— Church or state—confessed little interest in the lot of the lower classes, everywhere the overwhelming majority of the population; not Voltaire or Montesquieu, not Raynal or Rousseau, not Lessing or Kant or von Haller or Goethe. Struensee perhaps in Denmark, and Beccaria in Milan; and Tom Paine and Priestley in England but they fled to America. No, as Immanuel Kant observed in his *Strife of the Faculties*, progress, "if it is to come, must come from above, not by the movement of things from the bottom to the top, but by the movement from the top to the bottom. . . . To expect to train men who can improve themselves by means of education of the youth in intellectual and moral culture, is hardly to be hoped for." Nor did the *philosophes* look to the community, or the body politic, to achieve social progress. After all, except in England, Sweden, and some of the Swiss cantons, there was, strictly speaking, no body politic—not, certainly, as there was in Massachusetts or in Pennsylvania. Progress was something to be achieved through enlightened despots, or members of royal academies, or through the *philosophes* themselves, not through the people.

To summarize a complex affair, the American conception of progress was not a matter of cultural refinement but of material welfare and of freedom, a matter of health, wealth, education, and freedom to worship, to marry, to move about from region to region, from profession to profession. It was—and long remained —a matter of milk for the children, meat on the table, a well-built house and a well-filled woodshed, cattle and sheep in the pastures and hay in the barn,

> Where every farmer reigns a little king,
> Where all to comfort, none to danger rise,
> Where pride finds few, but nature all supplies,
> Where peace and sweet civility are seen . . .
> Where . . . round me rise
> A central school house, dress'd in modest guise!
> Where every child for useful life prepares,
> To business molded ere he knows its cares:
> In worth matures, to independence grows,
> And twines the civic garland o'er his brows
> > Timothy Dwight,
> > *Greenfield Hill* (1794)

Franklin and Paine, characteristically American both of them, will serve as archetypes of philosophers of progress. No one more confident of progress than Franklin, who thought of it, always, in practical terms. It meant better lighting, paved streets, newspapers, an efficient stove and an efficient government, peace with the Indians. It meant the Junto library and the College of Philadelphia and the American Philosophical Society. It meant the Albany Plan of Union and the Articles of Confederation and the Constitution. It meant moral progress, to be sure, but that too was a practical ideal, whether regulated by the famous score box

26

with the round dozen moral virtues that were to be cultivated by "habitude," or by new standards of international relations. Franklin did not aim at perfection: he did not suppose that Pennsylvania was Utopia, but he tried to make it less class ridden, less corrupt, less barbarous in its treatment of the Indian, and he succeeded.

There is no formal treatise on progress in the American literature of this era, but *The Rights of Man* comes closer to this than anything else, closer, certainly, than Joel Barlow's *Columbiad*, which purports to unfold (in 6,000 lines) before the enraptured gaze of Columbus a vision of the progress which would eventually encompass the world. Tom Paine had not only grand ideas about the future of man and civilization, but a specific program for the advancement of material well-being and social justice. "Establish the rights of man," he wrote,

> enthrone equality, form a good constitution, let there be no privileges, no distinctions of birth, no monopolies; make safe the liberty of industry and of trade, the equal distribution of family inheritance, publicity of administration, freedom of the press. These things established you will be assured of good laws.

These things established you will be sure of progress.

There was one test of progress on which philosophers, economists, and statesmen on both sides of the ocean were agreed; that was the test of population. "I am constantly astonished," wrote Rousseau, "that people should fail to recognize . . . a sign that is so simple. What is the purpose of political association? It is the preservation of prosperity of its members. And what is the most certain sign that they are prospering? It is the number and increase of population."

Here was, indeed, the incontrovertible test, and by this test the Old World did badly. There were improvements, to be sure, in the second half of the century, thanks to the potato, thanks to inoculation. But during the eighteenth century population over large areas of Europe—Spain, Portugal, and many of the Italian states—barely held its own. In Paris—the figures are from Buffon —10,000 out of 24,000 babies died during their first five years. In London the figure was even higher, and the magisterial Dr. Price presented figures which proved that there were 135 deaths for every 100 births in Berlin and no less than 169 deaths per 100 births in prosperous Amsterdam. Everywhere the story was the same—five out of twelve children born in the great cities died before they reached the age of five! During the third quarter of the century Copenhagen lost population three years out of every four, and even the population of rural Jutland declined. Elsewhere the prospect was not so bleak. Sweden increased its population by two-thirds during the century; Britain (including Ireland), Hungary, Bohemia, and Finland almost doubled.

But look at America. Everywhere from Maine to Georgia the story was the same: Americans were obeying the Biblical injunction to multiply and replenish the earth. There population doubled not in a century but every twenty or twenty-five years—the estimates vary, but roughly within these limits. Franklin demonstrated that the population of Pennsylvania doubled in twenty years, Jefferson that the population of Virginia, including slaves, doubled in twenty-seven years; Jeremy Belknap recorded that, notwithstanding the ravages of the war, the population of New Hampshire more than doubled between 1770 and 1790. Soon, what with Dr. Rush's *Medical Inquiries,* and Benjamin Smith Barton's observations on the progress of population, and Dr. William Currie's *Historical Account of the Climates and Diseases of the United States,* and Noah Webster's *Brief History of Epidemic and Pestilential Diseases,* and the speculations of historians like Samuel Williams and Hugh Williamson, American scientists were almost as busy with demography as is the Sixième Section today though—consider the Reverend Edward Wigglesworth's confident prediction of a population of 1,280,000,000 by the year 2000—not quite as cautious. And not only did population double every quarter century, but the whole of America was a kind of fountain of youth, where men and women lived, if not forever, at least well past the span allotted them by the Bible. It was a product of a salubrious climate, to be sure, but climate was more than physical environment, more than abundance of land and variety of soil and fecundity of animal life; it was a product of the social system where mothers could stay home and nurse their babies; it was the product of a religious system where the Church did not wrest tithes out of an impoverished peasantry; it was the product of a benevolent political system which encouraged freedom; it was a product of simplicity, innocence, and purity of morals. None put this better than Hugh Williamson, whose *History of North Carolina* meets most of the qualifications of modern cultural anthropology:

> The very consciousness of being free excites a spirit of enterprise and gives a spring to the intellectual faculties. If I could speak of our liberties as we speak of the climate and face of the country; if I could speak of their duration as we speak of things that are permanent in nature: I should venture with confidence to predict that in the scale of science the American states, in a few ages, would not shrink from a comparison with the Grecian republics, or any other people recorded in history.

*

We do not commonly think of James Monroe as a spokesman for the Enlightenment, and I have managed so far without invoking his name. Yet he was a product of the same Virginia, the same William and Mary, the same revolutionary fervor, that nourished Jefferson, and he lived all his life in the shadow of Monticello. Let me conclude with a passage from his first inaugural address, which came almost at the close of the American Enlightenment, a passage which sums up much of the thinking of that Enlightenment, and which has now, alas, an elegiac quality:

> Never did a government commence under auspices so favorable, nor ever was success so complete. If we look to the history of other nations, ancient or modern, we find no example of a growth so rapid, so gigantic, of a people so prosperous, and happy. In contemplating what we have still to perform, the heart of every citizen must expand with joy when he reflects how near our government has approached to perfection: that in respect to it we have no essential improvement to make, that the great object is to preserve it in the essential principles and features which characterize it, and that that is to be done by preserving the virtue and enlightening the minds of the people.

2

JEFFERSON
AND THE
ENLIGHTENMENT

I T was sometime in late September of 1780 that François Barbé de Marbois, newly appointed Secretary to the French Minister in Philadelphia (the Chevalier de la Luzerne), forwarded to governors and other dignitaries in each of the American States a list of twenty-two queries designed to provide him—or his government—with information about the new United States that might prove interesting and instructive. He was—as General John Sullivan observed—"one of those useful geniuses who is constantly in search of knowledge." Now it was America he wanted to know about; he had, after all, married an American girl; and he planned to cast in his lot with this new republic which fascinated him, as it fascinated so many of his fellow-countrymen. Only two of the many recipients of his inquiry bothered to answer him: General Sullivan, who eventually sent in a somewhat desultory response, and Thomas Jefferson, who had some claim to be considered the busiest man in the nation, but who found time to provide over three hundred pages of answers.

Mons. Marbois's questions covered geography, geology, natural resources, population, the native races, government, law, the economy, the military, religion, education, and a miscellany of marginal matters such as commerce and money, weights and measures, and even, for good measure, history. A big order this, comprehensive rather than searching, for it was information that Mons. Marbois wanted, rather than commentary, the kind of information the *philosophes* soaked up like a sponge, and then organized in vast dictionaries and encyclopedias or, perhaps, in philosophical histories.

That was a pretty busy winter for Governor Jefferson, and an anxious one, too. That October an enemy fleet sailed into Cape Henry and debouched General Leslie with several thousand red-coats on both shores of the James. The state seemed incapable of defending itself, and it was only good luck that took Leslie away from Virginia for more serious fighting in the Carolinas. The next month brought a more dangerous threat: the "parricide," Benedict Arnold, invaded Virginia, laying waste all the way to Richmond. Once again the state seemed helpless, and in December Arnold was back with further devastation. That spring of 1781 was one of the most difficult of Jefferson's life. His baby daughter, Lucy Elizabeth, died, and his beloved wife was sorely ill; his private affairs were in disorder; his estates were in ruins. At the same time the people of Virginia, sorely beset by a series of invasions which culminated in the massive invasion by Cornwallis, were distraught and desperate; the government of the Commonwealth was paralyzed. Conscious no doubt of the sorry role it had played in these crises, the Assembly now sought a scapegoat in Governor Jefferson. In May it retired to Charlottesville, and Jefferson, his term drawing to an end, took up residence in his beloved Monticello, where he could contemplate the ruin of his estates, and of so many of his hopes. The first week in June, Cornwallis sent Colonel Tarleton on a lightning raid designed to capture Mr.—no longer Governor—Jefferson, and the legislature. All escaped. After the Tarleton caper, Jefferson returned to his other home, Poplar Forest; on one of his daily rides around

34

the farm, his horse threw him to the ground, and he was, for some weeks, incapacitated. It is to that horse that we owe the compilation of the *Notes on Virginia.*

For Jefferson, who never wasted a moment, and whose schedule for his daughter Patsy left no time for play, or even for meals, employed some of his enforced leisure by returning to what he had originally welcomed but put aside in the press of events: the inquiries of Mons. Marbois, and the speculations they inspired. A welcome diversion these inquiries, for they touched a responsive chord.

By Christmas 1781 Jefferson had finished what he considered desultory Notes, and forwarded them to his friend, Charles Thomson, with the modest hint that they might be of interest to the Philosophical Society, of which Thomson was a kind of perpetual secretary. Mysteriously enough the Society did not respond, though Thomson himself did. "This country," he wrote, "affords to philosophic view an extensive, rich and unexplored field. It abounds in roots, plants, trees and minerals to the virtues and uses of which we are as yet stranger. . . . The mind of man is just awakening from a long stupor of many ages, to the discovery of useful arts and inventions. Our governments are yet unformed, and capable of great improvement. The history, manners, and customs of the aborigines are but little known. . . ."

"The philosophic view," that is what Marbois's inquiries excited and what Jefferson found irresistible—Jefferson who was even then contemplating a shift from public life to the life of the mind. Only a few weeks after he had received Mons. Marbois's letter he acknowledged—this time to his Italian friend, Charles Bellini—"the mysterious obligation for making me much better acquainted with my own country than I ever was before." That was scarcely possible, for no one knew Virginia better than this son of a surveyor who, since boyhood, had made its geography and resources, its people and society, its history and institutions his ceaseless concern, and who had built up, over the years, an incomparable private archive of the natural and civil history of the Commonwealth. "I had always made it a practice," he recalled later, "of obtaining any information of our country [he meant Virginia, of course], which might be of use to me in my station, public or private, and to commit it to writing." Even by 1780 his accumulation was formidable, for he kept records of everything—weather, the garden, the crops, the household economy; his travels, Indian vocabularies, judicial decisions, and colonial statutes; the letters he wrote and received, the books he bought and read, the buildings he admired and measured, the vineyards whose products he sampled, the mechanical contrivances he studied or invented. He was an inveterate collector, but there was nothing of the antiquarian about him; his records and collections were for use, as his reading, his writing, his very speculations, were for use.

Notes on Virginia—the informal title Jefferson gave to his book —was far more than Mons. Marbois had bargained for. It was, on one level, a guide book, even an encyclopedia; it was on another level a polemic—a refutation of the libels and canards that so many Europeans hurled at America—and on still a higher level, a philosophical inquiry, an interpretation, and a platform. It discussed not only government but the nature of government, not only education but the purpose of education, not only the statistics of native races and the economy of Negro slavery, but sociological problems of uniformity or differentiation in mankind, and moral problems of race and of slavery. Like Crèvecoeur's *Letters of An American Farmer* it both probed and illuminated the American character. And—though only by implication—it presented more fully than any other treatise of its day what might be called the agenda of the American Enlightenment.

*

It was a typical Enlightenment inquiry, this by Barbé-Marbois on the geography, the minerals, the cascades and caverns, the counties and townships, the weights and measures, of Virginia, for with these it mingled questions about "all that can increase the progress of human knowledge," "the administration of justice," "the different religions," and "the customs and manners" of the people. It was, on the surface, direct and unpretentious, but every *philosophe*, on both sides of the water, knew how to deal with this sort of thing: after all, just consider what the *philosophes* did with the innocuous and unambiguous subjects assigned them in the great Encyclopédie! *Notes on Virginia* takes its place, effortlessly, in the mainstream of Enlightenment literature: the literature that addressed itself to the exploration of Climate, or the interaction of Nature and Man, and the literature that embraced Civilization, or the social, political, and moral institutions of Man. It belongs with Buffon's great *Histoire Naturelle*—thirty-four volumes no less—which embraced the whole of Nature and of Man; with Father Lafitau's stunning volumes on the *Customs and Manners of the Savages of America;* with the Abbé Raynal's spectacular *Philosophical Inquiry into the History of the East and the West Indies* in eight impressive volumes; with George Forster's wonderful *Voyage Around the World;* with Crèvecoeur's *Letters of an American Farmer*—all of them philosophical contributions to the study of environment; it belongs, equally, with Montesquieu's *Spirit of the Laws*, Adam Smith's *Inquiry into the Wealth of Nations*, Voltaire's *Essay on the Customs and the Spirit of Nations*, Herder's dense study of the *Ideas on the History of Humanity*, and, at the end of the epoch, Madame de Stael's luminous essay on *Germany*. All of these inquiries were scientific, all were sociological, all were, eventually, moral; for the *philosophes* were natural philosophers, they were social philosophers, they were moral philosophers, and none more unequivocally than Jefferson.

Let us begin our study of Jefferson, then, with this matter of Climate, one of the master ideas of the Enlightenment. *The Notes* open almost artlessly, with "an exact description of the boundaries of Virginia" and with notices of "its rivers and mountains, its cascades and its caverns"; yet Jefferson manages to suffuse with poetry and to illuminate with philosophy even this prosaic record. Listen to his description of the passage of the Potomac through the Blue Ridge: "The distant finishing which Nature has given to the picture . . . is a true contrast to the foreground. It is as placid and delightful as that is wild and tremendous. For the Mountain being cloven asunder, she presents to your eye, through the cleft, a small catch of smooth blue horizon, at an infinite distance in the plain country, inviting you, from the riot and tumult roaring around, to pass through the breach and participate of the calm below." And of the Natural Bridge—for which he had pride of possession—"It is impossible for the emotions arising from the sublime to be felt beyond what they are here; so beautiful an arch, so elevated, so light, and springing as it were up to heaven. The rapture of the spectator is indescribable." From *Robinson Crusoe* and Haller's epic poem, *The Alps*, to the poems of Ossian and the *Sorrows of Werther*, the Enlightenment carried with it so much of the Romantic that we must conclude some infusion of Romanticism essential; nowhere—not even in Goethe—is the admixture more pronounced than in the Jefferson who planted his Palladian Monticello on the brow of a hill looking westward across a limitless wilderness, sat up all night with the Marquis de Chastellux reciting the *Odes* of Ossian (Ossian fraudulent enough, but not the enthusiasm he inspired), adored the noble savage Chief Logan of the Mingoes, confessed that music was the "dearest passion" of his life, and combined reason and romance in the *Notes on Virginia.*

It is when Jefferson turns to the description of quadrupeds and Man in the New World that the argument of Climate gathers

38

force, and more than force—that it becomes part of the great Enlightenment controversy over the role of Climate in civilization, and over the New World. Here, as in so many of his speculations, Jefferson gave a new dimension to the Enlightenment theory of Climate, one as yet unexplored by Old World Naturalists or philosophers. For in presenting the native races of Virginia, Jefferson was fairly confronted by that curious theory of New World degeneracy which had the support not only of malicious scribblers like the notorious Corneille de Pauw ("a mere compiler who read the writings of travelers only to repeat their lies," said Jefferson), but of a formidable galaxy of historians, sociologists, and naturalists, among them the crusading pamphleteer Abbé Raynal, the distinguished historian William Robertson of Edinburgh, and the Lord of all creation the Comte de Buffon. These, and others, accepted—for a time anyway—the argument that America had been doomed, by nature itself, to degeneracy. For it was in very truth a new world, one which had emerged later from the Flood than had the other continents, which was still afflicted with dismal swamps, impenetrable forests, and desperate extremes of heat and cold; a melancholy region where

nature remains concealed under her old garment and never exhibits herself in fresh attire. Being neither cherished nor cultivated by man, she never opens her beneficent womb. In this abandoned condition everything languishes, corrupts and proves abortive. The air and the earth, overloaded with humid and noxious vapors, are unable to purify themselves or to profit by the influence of the sun, which darts in vain his most enlivening rays upon this frigid mass.

Not only animals and plants, but Man himself degenerated in this inhospitable clime, for the noxious air and the poisonous soil do not sustain more than a sparse and miserable population. "The least vigorous European," wrote De Pauw, "is more

than a match for the strongest American." Feeble, indolent, slug-
gish, without strength or courage, without ardor for the female,
unable to reproduce themselves, the natives of America scarcely
deserve the name of men!

One might have supposed that a theory so palpably false would
not require refutation. Not at all. It had, after all, for its basis the
elementary fact that the vast area from the Rio Grande to the
Hudson's Bay did not support a population as large as that of
Ireland; it had for its incentive the risk that the same climate that
condemned the natives of America to degeneracy would work
havoc on European immigrants; it had for its moral support the
fact that the New World countenanced slavery; it had for its
animus fear of the loss of population to the New World and fear
of rivalry by the New World.

Scores of Americans rallied to refute these canards, but first
and last it was Jefferson who formulated the grand strategy of the
campaign and directed the tactics, and whose *Notes on Virginia*
delivered the decisive counterstroke. His method was that of the
Declaration, a combination of rhetoric and inductive reasoning;
here as in the Declaration Jefferson established a philosophical
position, and then submitted "facts . . . to a candid world." Here
are the facts, exact, comprehensive, and conclusive. Are American animals enfeebled and degenerate? Let us measure them. Let
us weigh the European and the American bear, the first a mere
153 pounds, the second 410 pounds. In Europe the beaver grew to
a maximum of eighteen pounds, in America to over forty. Or look
at the European deer, or renne, a mere three feet high; why we
will show you a moose from the forest of Maine that stands seven
feet, and the spread of his magnificent antlers is twice that of his
European cousins. Or contemplate the American bison of almost
two thousand shaggy pounds, or the bullock, of over 2,500
pounds, or the hog—why Jefferson himself had seen one that
weighed a thousand pounds! What has Europe to compare with

this? And because Jefferson knew that visible evidence was more persuasive than verbal, he followed up his arguments with demonstrations. Soon he was in Paris, soon he was inundating the Comte de Buffon with specimens of the American beaver, the American eagle, a brace of pheasants, the skin of a panther, the horns of a caribou, an elk and a roebuck. The search for a moose with which to confound Buffon reached epic proportions, with General Sullivan leading a mid-winter expedition into the Maine wilderness to track down a bull moose whose majestic size would confound the Count and forever silence all aspersions on nature in America. It was successful, too: the moose which Sullivan shipped over to the *Jardin de Roi*—at Jefferson's expense of course —converted even the reluctant Count.

Even more eloquent was Jefferson's vindication of the native races—more eloquent and more far-reaching in its implications. How the primitive fascinated the Enlightenment: cultural anthropology was in a sense an invention of the eighteenth-century *philosophes* and explorers, like Lafitau and Mallet and George Forster, and of the Americans, too. Men were after all everywhere the same. Undress them, literally and figuratively, and the similarity was palpable—in the courts of Europe or on the shores of the Huron, in civilized China or on an island paradise in the South Pacific; and if there was nobility, it was to be found not at Versailles or Vienna, but among the savages. There were differences, to be sure, but they were differences imposed not by nature, but by social and cultural conditions. Back then to original man, sail to Tahiti to find some Omai who could be transported to England to titillate the ladies of the court; penetrate the forests of Canada and find some Adario running wild in the woods, just as Dryden had described him; unveil him in the mists of Iceland, a fierce Viking with more heroism and more poetry than in any people since the days of the Trojan wars; recover him among the remnants of the once proud Incas in some remote mountain fastness in Peru; or resurrect him from the ruins of the ancient world, "so full of beautiful and godlike and youthful forms."

This was mostly moonshine as every American knew; the truth was somewhere between the mendacities of a De Pauw and the romantic imaginings of the Baron Lahontan, who had invented Adario, or Father Lafitau who was sure that the Hurons were the descendants of the Trojans and the Greeks. The truth was indeed to be found in America, and among the Indians with whom Europeans had been familiar for two centuries. Formally, or informally—and mostly the latter—all the American philosophers were ethnologists: Franklin who had made treaties with the Indians, and Governor Cadwallader Colden of New York who wrote on the Five Civilized Tribes, and Washington who had fought them, and John Bartram who had lived with them, and Charles Thomson, Secretary to the Philosophical Society who was adopted into the Delaware tribe, and Dr. Rush who speculated so audaciously about their physical and mental characteristics, and Crèvecoeur who saw their best and their worst qualities. None knew them better than Jefferson, or had studied more assiduously their character and their history; over the years he had collected some fifty Indian vocabularies, a priceless collection lost to vandalism. No one contributed more to our knowledge of them, directly through the *Notes on Virginia*, indirectly through sponsoring such explorers as the Yankee John Ledyard, whom Jefferson launched on his astonishing pedestrian expedition from Paris to Kamchatka, and who was prepared to prove, from personal experience, the unity of the natives of Siberia and of the American West; or André Michaux who combined botanizing with ethnology, and a bit of diplomacy too; or Meriwether Lewis and William Clark whose famous expedition was one of the glories of the Jefferson Administration; or

Albert Gallatin, who was Jefferson's disciple and successor as an ethnologist.

Now, in the *Notes*, Jefferson seized the opportunity to demonstrate that the Old World animadversions on the Indian were as misguided as those on nature. The Indian was a product of Climate, and, over the ages, had adapted himself perfectly to that Climate. He was ardent and brave, strong and agile, resourceful and sagacious, perfectly adapted to the nature which produced him. As for ardor and virility, the Indians have the passions and the powers that the circumstances of their lives dictate, neither more nor less, and their bodies and minds are as well adapted to their environment as are the bodies and minds of Europeans to the environment of civilization. And with this went eloquence, and nobility of character. To demonstrate these qualities, Jefferson reproduced the speech of Chief Logan of the Mingoes, a flight of eloquence worthy of Demosthenes himself—or perhaps we should say of Jefferson, for we cannot wholly resist the suspicion that it was all more Jefferson than Logan.

If Climate was decisive, then logically the animadversions of Buffon and Raynal and De Pauw extended to all who were the victims of that climate, Europeans as well as natives; Raynal and De Pauw embraced this logic. "The Creoles, though educated at the Universities of Mexico and Lima," wrote De Pauw, "have never produced a single book, and through the whole length of America, from Cape Horn to the Hudson Bay, there has never appeared a philosopher, an artist, a man of learning whose name has found a place in the history of science or whose talents have been of any use to others." You might ignore De Pauw, but what do you say to the learned Dr. Robertson, Rector of the University of Edinburgh, and author of a famous *History of the Americas:* "The same qualities in the climate of America which stunted the growth . . . of its native animals proved pernicious to such as have migrated into it voluntarily." What do you say to the Abbé Raynal? "How astonishing it is that America has not yet produced a single good poet, or able mathematician, or a man of genius in any one of the arts or the sciences." The charge—which was to resound again and again in the next half-century—was absurd on the face of it, and Jefferson might well have disdained it. Instead he disposed of it with two characteristic thrusts. First—indulging his passion for calculating—he pointed out that America, "though but a child of yesterday," had produced, in a single generation, a Washington, a Franklin, a Rittenhouse (and, he might have added, a Jefferson). "We calculate thus," he wrote: "The United States contains three millions of inhabitants; France twenty millions, and the British islands ten. France then should have produced half a dozen of each, and Great Britain half that number, equally eminent." Clearly neither had done so. More interesting was Jefferson's second argument: that Americans had not only made striking contributions to government, philosophy, and war, but had "given hopeful proofs of genius of the nobler kinds, which arouse the best feelings of man, which call him into action, which substantiate his freedom, and conduct him to happiness." Here is the Jeffersonian test of civilization— not power, not even philosophy and culture—but freedom and happiness.

All of this was a stunning refutation of the denigrations of a Buffon, a Raynal, of all those who argued the natural inferiority of the New World to the Old. Far from being degenerate, feeble, enervated, without talent or genius, the inhabitants of the New World were the most fortunate of men, and the New World environment was the most favorable of any in the western world. It was blessed by every climate and every soil; there Nature produced the most abundant of crops, the tallest of trees, the most numerous, largest, and most varied forms of bird and animal life of all climates. It was most favorable to the health and happiness of man. This was a theme to which Jefferson returned again and again for half a century—the infinite superiority, natural as well as social, of the New World to the Old. This was neither provincialism nor chauvinism—though Jefferson confessed a touch of both; it was simply the fact of the matter.

For what was the test of a successful civilization that was universally acknowledged in the eighteenth-century world; what but the test of population?

To Mons. Marbois's query about population, Jefferson gave due attention in the *Notes;* it was a subject to which he returned again and again, as did all the American *philosophes.* The Abbé Raynal himself had made clear the central significance of population:

> But it will be asked, whether a great degree of population is of use to promote the happiness of mankind. This is an idle question. In fact the point is not to multiply men in order to make them happy; but it is sufficient to make them happy, that they should multiply.

And no wonder that the elder Mirabeau's book, *L'Ami des Hommes,* should display a subtitle, *A Treatise on Population.*

By this test—and none had any misgivings about it—few Old World peoples could claim to be happy. But look at America: at the beginning of the century the English colonies counted less than 400,000 inhabitants; sixty years later their number had increased five-fold, and when they took the first census in 1790 they counted four million. Nor was this the product of immigration, though that, too, was a tribute to the attraction of the New World. It was, as Benjamin Franklin had pointed out, "the salubrity of the air, the healthiness of the Climate, the Plenty of good provisions, the Encouragement of early Marriages by the certainty of Subsistence in cultivating the Earth." It was more: it was the beneficent nourishment of a climate of freedom, of enlightenment, of virtue. Soon everyone was a demographer, estimating the rate of increase of population and correlating it with the happiness and welfare of man. And how impressive the agreement among them: all came to the same conclusion, Franklin, Jefferson, Dr. Rush, Dr. Currie, William Smith Barton—all of them members of the Philosophical Society circle in Philadelphia —that in America population doubled every twenty or twenty-five years. What a prospect for the future! Jefferson himself predicted a population of four and one-half million for Virginia by the year 1860, even without immigration which, oddly enough, he thought dangerous to the republican experiment. And he noted, with a curious mixture of pride and illogic, that so favorable was the American environment that even the slave population kept pace with the free.

As Dr. Barton concluded, "Must not the mind of every American citizen be impressed with gratitude and glow with emotions of a virtuous pride, when he reflects on the blessings his country enjoys?" That was, indeed, the Jeffersonian thesis: that a population which flourished and increased was both a product of and a tribute to the blessings which America enjoyed—blessings not only of Nature, but of government, economy, and society.

Oddly enough—for Marbois was familiar with, and not unsympathetic to, the teachings of Quesnay and Turgot and Du Pont and the Abbé Morellet, and the other economists who made up what Du Pont called the Physiocratic school—not one of the twenty-two queries which were submitted to Mr. Jefferson concerned agriculture. No matter, Jefferson did not feel himself bound by the letter or the order of the queries, but used them as points of departure for what he wished to say. And here was Query 19: "The Present State of Manufactures, Commerce, Interior and Exterior Trade?" After all Virginia had no manufacturers, and precious little commerce or trade, none really except for trade in tobacco, something of a calamity, that. Jefferson seized upon the question to discuss what was central to his philosophy and close to his heart—agriculture.

Just as "natural philosophy," in the vocabulary of the eighteenth century, stood for the whole of science, and "climate" for the total environment, so "agriculture" was more than farming, it was a way of life. This was the truth that the Physiocrats had caught and made central to their philosophy—that an agricultural economy was the only one that conformed to the dictates of nature and nature's God; avoided the evils of colonies and wars and exorbitant taxes that plagued governments, and of misery and luxury and vice that were the concommitants of great cities; added real wealth to the Commonwealth and nourished and safeguarded the virtue of men and society.

It was one of the great issues of the day, that between mercantilism and physiocracy. Like the controversies between Reason and Faith, the Ancients and the Moderns, Civilization and the Primitive, Progress and Happiness, it connected itself with almost every aspect of life, and spread out from its economic center to embrace great questions of politics, sociology, and morals. It went to the very heart of the issue that divided most of the *philosophes* from the rulers: What was the center of gravity: the power and prosperity of the state or the happiness and liberty of man? The mercantilists, and their allies the Cameralists, such as Frederick the Great in the Old World and Hamilton in the New, were prepared to subordinate everything to the prosperity of the state; this was the policy the rulers of France, Spain, Russia, Sweden, and (though Joseph II was dazzled by the Physiocrats) of the Empire. These strove to be self-sufficient, which meant control of the economy at home and abroad; a ceaseless struggle for colonies and for the mastery of trade to the far corners of the globe; armies, navies, merchant shipping, and taxation to support all this—all the things that the Abbé Raynal had exposed in his *History of the European Establishments in the East and West Indies.* The Physiocrats and their allies—and they had allies everywhere,

47

Joseph in Vienna and Charles in Baden and Struensee in Denmark, and Adam Smith in Edinburgh and Filangieri down in Naples—knew that wealth, like virtue and happiness, was rooted in conformity with nature and that, in the last analysis, it was only the cultivation of the soil that was truly natural. They abjured great cities, colonies, the search for exotic products which led to slavery and all its evils, the panoply of armies and navies, courts and palaces, with their inevitable accompaniment of luxury and extravagance. They celebrated the simple life.

Morally the Physiocrats had the best of the argument; Raynal made that quite clear in his History which was a moral tract as well as an economic, tracing most of the evils of the age—such as slavery and the slave trade—to the insensate search for wealth by individuals and power by governments. But in the Old World, alas, the Physiocrats came too late; history had baked their cake. They came too late to change the pattern of politics, too late to reverse the tides of history; too late to change the minds of men. The great cities were there, draining off the best of the countryside, spreading social and moral ruin, just as Hogarth depicted, just as Fielding made clear; the kings and princes were there, determined to strengthen the state—and themselves—at all hazards, greedy for territory, colonies, and markets; the great merchant companies were there, exploiting backward peoples, draining the wealth from distant lands to fatten the fortunes of princes and nabobs; the armies and the navies were there, eager for glory and spoils, and spreading devastation where they went; the courts and the palaces were there, breeding places for luxury and vice; the remnants of feudalism were there too—and not always just the remnants, witness Russia, Hungary, Denmark, Spain, Bourbon Italy, Poland—or what was left of it. No wonder the Physiocrats were frustrated or put to flight: Turgot forced out of office, the Emperor Joseph driven to embrace Cameralism, Struensee, who had tried to reverse the Bernstorff mercantilist policy,

48

beheaded, and even in England the magnanimous Shelburne forced to give way to the narrow Sheffield.

But America presented a very different scene and one which offered the most exhilarating prospect to all those who believed in the moral superiority of agriculture and the rural life. There everything was precisely what the Physiocrats prescribed: a boundless territory with—as Jefferson said in his First Inaugural Address—"land enough for our descendants to the thousandth and thousandth generation," and land, too, of unrivaled fecundity; a staunch yeomanry (look aside from slavery, a curse which almost all the American *philosophes* hoped to root out), every one —according to Crèvecoeur—independent and happy; no feudal remnants for, with Jefferson leading the way, the new nation rid itself of these; no great cities, no manufacturers, no colonies—for the territories west of the mountains were not to be territories but commonwealths; no great military to eat up the substance of the people, or subvert their government; no ecclesiastical establishment to claim tithes or aggrandize land. And, on top of all this, Americans were "kindly separated by Nature and a wide ocean from the exterminating havoc of one quarter of the globe" and "too high-minded to endure the degradations of others"—it is of course Jefferson who is speaking, Jefferson who all his life counseled isolation from the political and moral contamination of the Old World.

All the New World was an experimental laboratory for physiocracy; nowhere was the laboratory more nearly ideal than in Virginia. It was, after all, the most populous of American states, and the largest, stretching as it did from the Ocean to the Mississippi: no Old World nation outside Russia had so imperial a domain! All of its people were farmers, slaves as well as masters, drawing their sustenance from the virtuous soil. It was ruled not by princes or absentee nabobs but by planters who lived on their farms and busied themselves with the welfare of the communities, every one a Cincinnatus, a Fabius or a Cato or, better yet, a Washington, a Wythe, a Madison—or a Jefferson; and those who were not planters were even more independent, for they were independent of the curse of slavery. Where was there a fairer prospect for the evolution of an agrarian republic? Where —not even excluding France—was there a spokesman more eloquent, a practitioner more skillful, or a statesman more effective than Jefferson?

Let us return to the *Notes* and listen to Jefferson weighing the issue of agriculture versus manufacturers.

> We have an immensity of land courting the industry of the husbandman. Is it best that all our citizens should be employed in its improvement, or that one half should be called off from that to exercise manufactures and handicraft arts for the other? Those who labor in the earth are the chosen people of God, if ever He had a chosen people, whose breasts He has made his peculiar deposit for substantial and genuine virtue. It is the focus in which He keeps alive that sacred fire, which otherwise might escape from the face of the earth. Corruption of morals in the mass of cultivators is a phenomenon of which no age nor nation has furnished an example. It is the mark set on those who, not looking up to heaven . . . for their subsistence, depend for it on casualties and caprice of customers. . . . Generally speaking, the proportion which the aggregate, which the other classes of citizens, bears in any state to that of its husbandmen, is the proportion of its unsound to its healthy parts.

Jefferson spent his life in public service, but he always counted himself a husbandman. He had inherited many acres, and acquired more through marriage; at the time he wrote the *Notes* he was owner of thirteen farms including his favorites, Monticello and Poplar Forest, and to the cultivation and improvement of these he gave his unflagging attention. Again and again, in his long life, he sought to abandon that public career which threatened to absorb all of his energies, and devote himself to that occupation which promised such rich rewards of contentment and the assurance of usefulness, but always, until 1809, in vain. "I have often thought," he wrote to the painter Charles Wilson Peale, "that if Heaven had given me choice of my position and calling, it should have been on a rich spot of earth, well watered, and near a good market for the productions of the garden. No occupation is so delightful to me as the culture of the earth, and no culture comparable to that of the garden," and his passion for the garden is lovingly recorded in the *Garden Book* which he kept faithfully through much of his life. The greatest service which anyone can render his country, he asserted in his Autobiography, is to add a new plant to its culture, and this he himself did in ample measure. He was indefatigable in his search for different varieties of rice and obtained seed from the Piedmont, Egypt, and even Sumatra. From Italy he imported the Lombardy poplar, soon to be almost as familiar in America as in France and Italy. In an effort to encourage the cultivation of the olive ("of all the gifts of Heaven to man it is, next to [bread] the most precious"), he shipped over more than five hundred olive trees—alas in vain. He experimented with figs from France, vetch from England, grapes and strawberries from Italy, endives from France, and silk trees from China and Constantinople. He visited the vineyards of the Loire, Bordeaux, the Moselle, and the Rhine, and encouraged viniculture in Virginia, and he instructed his old friend Philip Mazzei (who had lived for some years at Monticello) to send him from Italy four vignerons each of whom could play a different musical instrument. Fascinated as he ever was with inventions and contrivances, he experimented with spinning machines, and with a new seed-box for sowing clover (which reduced the cost from six shillings to two shillings an acre), built and perfected a hemp-breaking machine, and was the first Virginian to import one of the new Scottish threshing machines

51

which, as usual, he improved. Most important of his inventions was the mouldboard plough, specifically designed for the soil of Virginia. Jefferson thought it "the finest plough ever constructed in America" and the Agricultural Society of Paris agreed with this verdict, and awarded it a gold medal. In all this, as he himself put it, he combined "a *theory* which may satisfy the learned, with a *practice* intelligible to the most unlettered laborer."

All these were, in a sense, private contributions, which Jefferson made simply as a farmer cooperating with other farmers, for even here he never kept to himself or for himself: he was even prepared to give ten guineas a year to pay an Italian orchardman to ship olive trees to America. Far more important were the public contributions:

Jeffersonian agrarianism was very different from the physiocracy of a Turgot or of his disciple, Du Pont de Nemours; it was pragmatic, not doctrinaire, democratic not exclusive. To Jefferson an air of unreality hung over much of the thinking of the *Économistes*—an unreality which was a product in part of their own abstract thinking, in part of the circumstances of the French society and economy. Thus Du Pont—of all the *Économistes* he was closest to Jefferson, and his correspondence the most illuminating—persuaded himself that as only those who labor in the earth are real members of the community, all others—he called them "inhabitants" rather than "citizens"—should be excluded from the suffrage.

> Municipal and sovereign rights [he wrote Jefferson], the right to sit and deliberate in political assemblies, that of voting, that of promulgating and executing the laws, belong exclusively to landowners, because these only are members of a particular republic. . . . When one believes that those who have naught but their two arms and their personal property are citizens just as much as the landowners are, one is aiding in the brewing of a storm, preparing the way for revolutions. (12 Dec. 1811.)

Worse yet, Du Pont went so far as to deplore the American practice of manhood suffrage. "You have kept the bad English laws, and all of England's bad customs," he reproved Jefferson; "one of the worst is the establishment of popular elections." But Jefferson's belief that those who labor in the earth are the peculiarly beloved of God did not lead him to exclude those who were not farmers or landholders from God's favor—or from the American agrarian paradise; his commitment to the principle that society was a contract which embraced all its members prevented that; his common sense prevented that.

Jefferson, indeed, had little more interest in or patience with doctrinaire *philosophes* like La Mettrie or Holbach or Mably than did John Adams, though he was far more discriminating than that irascible critic. It was, in the end, the *Ideologues* whom Jefferson most admired—Condillac, Cabanis, Destutt de Tracy, and the other members of that fascinating school who most vigorously carried on the traditions of Lockean sensationalism, rooted them firmly in biology and zoology, and applied them—somewhat less firmly—to politics, economics, education, and morals. Here he was, in a sense (or at least by analogy), an American Turgot, able to carry through on the most favorable theater the kind of program that Turgot was unable to carry through in France.

Once again we are in the presence of the most pervasive pattern of the American Enlightenment, and one which Jefferson represented better than did any of his countrymen: the pattern of Old World formulation and New World actualization of Enlightenment principles. Nowhere, except in the realm of religion and the Church, is this pattern more ostentatious than in the realm of what was coming to be called Political Economy—a concept which embraced such diverse interests as agriculture, commerce, finance, politics—domestic and imperial—demography, and sociology. To the philosophical foundations of Political Economy, the Americans made but meager contributions. They felt no need for philosophy; what they did was, quite simply, "to realize the theories of the wisest writers." Here, as elsewhere in the American Enlightenment, philosophy was the product of circumstances rather than the other way around, a recognition of an existing condition. The more formal and sophisticated rationalization of agrarianism—as with Jefferson's disciple, John Taylor of Carolina—came only in response to the Hamiltonian challenge, and even then it was argued rather as the common sense of the matter than as a body of scientific principles.

In Paris Jefferson gravitated almost instinctively to the salons of the Duc de la Rochefoucauld and of the Comtesse d'Houdetot, frequented by the *Economistes* and their friends. A great swell, La Rochefoucauld, but indubitably a *philosophe;* he had worshiped Dr. Franklin, and counted Lafayette and Condorcet his closest friends, and to demonstrate the American political genius he had translated all the American constitutions into elegant French. Even more agreeable was the salon of the Comtesse d'Houdetot; she was the Julie of Rousseau's *New Heloise* and of the *Confessions,* too, published even as Jefferson was in France; there Jefferson met the Abbé Morellet, who was to translate his *Notes on Virginia,* and Crèvecoeur, fresh from the horrors of the American war, but still faithful to his ideal of the American Farmer, and Jean François Marmontel, author of the notorious *Belisaire* and historiographer-royal, and Condorcet and his young disciple Du Pont de Nemours who edited the journal of the Physiocrats, and who was shortly to become Jefferson's disciple. It was for the Comtesse's garden at Sannois that Jefferson ordered a large shipment of trees, shrubs, and flowers from America.* The American Minis-

*See Edwin Betts, *Garden Book,* 146–47 for list; see also Chinard, *Les Amities Americaines de Madame d'Houdetot,* p. 1924.

ter did not need to go to school to these Physiocrats, but doubtless he was gratified to find so many *philosophes* eager to put into practice in France what he could take for granted in Virginia and perhaps in the whole of America.

For almost alone of the great agrarians of that era, Jefferson stood not in the shadow of power but at the center of power. As a member of the Virginia legislature he took the lead in abolishing those remnants of feudalism—primogeniture and entail—and his program of Disestablishment carried with it the ultimate forfeiture of the glebe lands of the Church. His proposal to grant fifty acres to every adult male who was landless was rejected, but where he failed in Virginia he succeeded on a vastly larger theater, for the purchase of Louisiana doubled the agricultural domain and, together with the liberal provisions of the Ordinances for organizing the transmontane West, guaranteed (for at least another generation) a flourishing agrarian republic. Jefferson had sought to link that guarantee with one prohibiting slavery in all the new western domain, but in this, too, he was frustrated. It was one of the ironies of Jefferson's career that the policies which contributed so richly to nourish agrarian democracy nourished too that institution of slavery which he regarded as the gravest evil and the gravest danger facing the republic. To its eradication Jefferson devoted much of his thought, his energies, and his emotions, too. He succeeded in ameliorating slavery, but not in ending it, and this failure he came to regard as irreparable. It was, needless to say, more than a personal failure; it was the most conspicuous failure of American democracy, it was the most conspicuous failure of the American Enlightenment.

Mons. Marbois had not inquired directly about slavery—was that an example of Gallic tact?—but Jefferson made room for a consideration of the tragic subject in replies to two marginal queries, one long, detailed, and analytical, the other short, general, and philosophical. Let us listen as Jefferson elaborates on "the particular customs and manners that may happen to be received" in Virginia:

There must doubtless be an unhappy influence on the manners of our people produced by the existence of slavery among us. The whole commerce between master and slave is a perpetual exercise of the most boisterous passions, the most unremitting despotism on the one part, and degrading submissions on the other. Our children see this and learn to imitate it. . . . The parent storms, the child looks on, catches the lineaments of wrath, puts on the same airs in the circle of smaller slaves, gives a loose to the worst of passions, and thus nursed, educated, and daily exercised in tyranny, cannot but be stamped by it with odious peculiarities. The man must be a prodigy who can retain his manners and morals undepraved by such circumstances. And with what execration should the statesman be loaded who, permitting one half the citizens to trample on the rights of the other, transforms those into despots, and these into enemies, destroys the morals of the one part and the *amor patriae* of the other. . . . With the morals of the people, their industry is also destroyed. For in a warm climate no man will labor for himself who can make another labor for him. . . . And can the liberties of a nation be thought secure when we have removed their only firm basis, a conviction in the minds of the people that these liberties are of the gift of God? That they are not to be violated but with His wrath. Indeed I tremble for my country when I reflect that God is just; that his justice cannot sleep forever; that considering numbers, nature and natural means only, a revolution of the wheel of fortune, an exchange of situation, is among possible events; that it may become probable by supernatural interference. The Almighty has no attribute which can take side with us in such a contest.

Here was the voice of the Enlightenment which, after Montesquieu, turned more and more against slavery and the slave trade. Though Denmark was the first nation to abolish the slave trade, it was the French who, more than any other, formulated the argument against slavery itself. Nowhere was the moral argument stated more eloquently than in the *Encyclopédie*—almost the official organ of the *philosophes:*

> There is not a single one of these hapless souls [wrote the Chevalier de Jaucourt of Negro slaves] who does not have the right to be declared free, since he has never lost his freedom; since it was impossible for him to lose it; and since neither his ruler nor his father nor any one else had the right to dispose of his freedom; consequently the sale of his person is null and void in and of itself. This Negro does not divest himself, indeed cannot under any condition divest himself, of his natural rights. He carries them everywhere with him, and has the right to demand that others permit him to enjoy those rights. It is therefore a clear case of inhumanity by judges in free countries to which the salve is shipped, not to free the slave instantly by legal declaration, since he is their brother, having a soul like theirs.

That was precisely what Lord Mansfield ruled in the famous Somersett case of 1772 and what Chief Justice Cushing of Massachusetts was to rule in the Quock Walker case a decade later. But that was not, alas, for Virginia.

Slavery troubled not only the conscience of the Enlightenment, but its philosophy and its logic. For in the eyes of the *philosophes* slavery was not merely a moral wrong; it was—as Jefferson made clear with his references to the attitude of the Almighty—a violation of the natural order of things. For it was one of the basic convictions of the Enlightenment that men were everywhere fundamentally the same, a conviction which implied equality, *in esse* or *in posse*. That was why it was so easy for the *philosophes* to draw so casually but so confidently on China and Peru, the Greeks and the Trojans, the Vikings and the Hurons, the nomads of Arabia Felix and the Gaelic bards of Ossian. That was why political philosophers assumed that men everywhere displayed the same passions, ambitions, zeal for power and for glory, and for tyranny, too, and that the conclusions which you drew from the history of Athens and Sparta and Rome were valid for France and England and America. That is why the hundreds of Utopias depicted men responding everywhere to the same persuasions of Reason and morality and self-interest. But if Nature had made all men the same, to exalt some as masters and condemn others to be slaves was quite simply to violate the laws of Nature.

Nor was there any room for the notion of the permanent inferiority of the Negro in the conception of the universe as a Great Chain of Being. That concept assumed an infinite hierarchy of beings, and in this hierarchy man—"a little less than angels, a little more than apes"—was one. How wisely Samuel Richardson admonished the readers of *Clarissa*,

> Nor let the rich the lowliest slave disdain,
> He's equally a link of nature's chain.

Everywhere the Enlightenment exalted Freedom—not that convulsive freedom of conduct for the individual that animated a Werther indulging his sorrows, a Beckford his eccentricities, an Alfieri his passions, a Gustavus III his vanities; but that larger freedom which a Voltaire, a Condorcet, a Priestley, a Jefferson celebrated—freedom to resist and overcome the pretensions of Authority, the audacities of Government, the fanaticism of the

Church, the superstitions of ignorance, the burdens of poverty, the paralysis of impotence; freedom from slavery in every form. And what form more ostentatious than that which flourished so incongruously in that new Republic which purported to vindicate the right to life, liberty, and the pursuit of happinesses?

At the time he published the *Notes on Virginia* no one had contributed more to the struggle against slavery in his own state, and perhaps even in the nation, than Jefferson, who was himself a large slaveholder, and whose private relationship to the peculiar institution was marked by those ambiguities almost inescapable in a southerner. As early as 1770, in his argument in the obscure case of Howell v. Netherland, which involved the freedom or enslavement of a third-generation Mulatto, Jefferson had pled that "we are all born free," and that slavery was contrary to nature—an argument which the court dismissed out of hand. Time did not reconcile Jefferson to the paradox of a society proclaiming freedom and perpetuating slavery, and six years later he tried, in vain, to identify the political rights of the Americans with the personal rights of Negro slaves. "He has waged cruel war against human nature"—so went Jefferson's original draft of the Declaration—"violating the most sacred rights of life and liberty in the persons of a distant people who never offended him, captivating them and carrying them into slavery in another hemisphere. . . . Determined to keep open a market where MEN could be bought and sold, he has prostituted his negative for suppressing every legislative attempt to prohibit or restrain this execrable commerce." The Continental Congress was not ready for either the sentiment or the rhetoric, and the passage was omitted. That fall Jefferson returned to the Virginia Assembly, where he promptly introduced a bill ending the importation of slaves, and two years later Virginia enacted the prohibition. Nor should we forget that it was President Jefferson who urged, and signed, the bill which, at the earliest moment permitted under the Constitution, permanently outlawed the importation of slaves to the United States.

That same fall of 1776 Jefferson introduced a bill for the complete revisal of the laws of Virginia; he was appointed to the committee responsible for the revisal and promptly seized the laboring oar. His proposed revisions—one hundred and twenty-six bills altogether—embraced the whole of the legal code: citizenship, land, crime, religion, education, and, inevitably, slavery. Here Jefferson submitted the bold proposal of emancipation for all Negroes born after 1800, with the provision that those born of slaves "should be brought up, at the public expense, to tillage, arts, or sciences according to their geniuses" and, when they reached maturity, colonized "to such place as circumstances should render most proper." This proposal rested on two assumptions: that "nothing is more certainly written in the book of Fate than that these people are to be free," and that it is not less certain "that the two races, equally free, cannot live in the same government." The first of these assumptions was characteristically optimistic; it was not Fate but War that brought freedom to the slave. The second was not only uncharacteristically pessimistic, but inconsistent with Enlightenment principles which emphasized what men had in common as members of the human race rather than what divided them by race or color. The proposal was, in any event, so radical that it was unacceptable and died in committee. "What a stupendous, what an incomprehensible, machine is man," wrote Jefferson to M. Demeusnier, whose article on America for the *Encyclopédie Methodique* Jefferson largely rewrote, "who can endure toil, famine, stripes, imprisonment and death itself in vindication of his own liberty, and the next moment be deaf to all those motives whose power supported him through his trial, and inflict on his fellow-men a bondage, one hour of which is fraught with more misery than ages of that which he rose in rebellion to oppose."

By now Jefferson had moved back from the state to the national arena, and had transferred to that arena the campaign against slavery, and it was here that he may have made his most significant contribution. As chairman of the congressional committee to provide government for the vast hinterland west of the Alleghenies, he tried to write into the Ordinance a clause prohibiting slavery in any of the territory after the year 1800. The proposal was lost by one vote; as Jefferson wrote Demeusnier, "The voice of a single individual . . . would have prevented this abominable crime from spreading itself over the new country. Thus we see the fate of millions unborn hanging on the tongue of one man, and Heaven was silent in that awful moment." All was not lost; three years later the Northwest Ordinance incorporated for all the territory north of the Ohio the principle Jefferson had attempted to apply to the entire West. And we should not forget that until the crisis of the fifties which (just as Jefferson foresaw) rent the Union apart, that principle applied to most of the vast Louisiana Territory which Jefferson had acquired for the nation in 1803.

Slavery resisted all pressures of the Enlightenment; in other areas the familiar pattern was vindicated: Old World theories became New World realities, Old World philosophies were translated into New World institutions. Clearly this was not because American *philosophes* were more effective, or more ingenious, than their Old World colleagues, but because their task was incomparably easier.

If the deepest and most pervasive commitment of the Enlightenment on both sides of the water was to Freedom, Jefferson spoke for them all—certainly for all his fellow countrymen—when he dedicated himself to the "illimitible freedom of the human mind." Though Americans did not win freedom for slaves, elsewhere they were more successful, and nowhere more than in that realm which was to the Old World what slavery was to the New—religion. Voltaire's great rallying cry, *Ecrasez l'infâme*, was the *cri de coeur* of the *philosophes* everywhere, even in liberal Britain where Catholics and Nonconformists were far from free. From London to St. Petersburg, from Stockholm to Naples, the Church was imperial, powerful, formidable, magisterial, and Established; everywhere it shared with the Crown power over the minds and the souls of men and—except in Holland—regarded the slightest rent in the web of conformity as not only morally, but politically pernicious. It controlled education in the schools, and, too, in the universities. It stopped the Encyclopédie for seven years, sending luckless writers to the Bastille and printers to the galleys. It dispensed justice and injustice, broke dissenters on the wheel or burned them at the stake. In Russia it exploited the labor of one million serfs, and in Poland one peasant out of every seven was a serf on church lands. Even in Enlightened England which Voltaire admired, it penalized all forms of nonconformity. Unitarians were required to take the Test Act oath; they were all—so Edmund Burke asserted—disciples of Tom Paine and against all religion; and Justice Sir William Scott insisted that the Quakers were so dangerous that they were "unworthy of legislative indulgence" of any kind. Nor was the power of the Church confined to the Old World: it dominated the political, economic, and intellectual life of Spanish America from Santiago to San Francisco, and even after the fall of Canada, the British, while they extended their own establishment to their new province, allowed the Catholic Church to retain most of its ancient authority.

Five of the American States inherited Anglican Establishments, and though these were mild enough in their pretensions and harmless enough in their conduct, they were—or to the

American *philosophes* they seemed—pernicious in principle.

Here as elsewhere Jefferson seized the lead in the struggle not merely to overthrow the Anglican Establishments, but to build something scarcely dreamed of in the philosophy of Old World radicals—"a wall of separation between Church and State."

It is hard for us now to appreciate the audacity of this proposal or the radicalism of the philosophy which dictated it. The *philosophes* of the Old World did not really want to wipe the religious slate clean. It was not the Establishment they assailed, but the conduct of the Establishment; not the power of the Church, but the abuse of that power. They were prepared, most of them, to settle for a well-behaved Establishment—for ending the Inquisition, expelling the Jesuits, confiscating some of the Church lands, lifting ecclesiastical censorship. Most of the Utopias which they constructed—and every *philosophe* had a Utopia in his pocket—provided for a state religion. Rousseau, who drew up model constitutions for Poland and Corsica, proposed that every citizen subscribe to his state religion or suffer exile or even death. The Abbé Mably in his *Phocion* called for a state religion and the outlawing of all new religions. The Abbé Robin, who had fought in America, called upon the United States to impose a common faith on all its people in order to assure national unity. And when Sebastian Mercier imagined his Utopia of *The Year 2440* he arranged for an established church, ecclesiastical censorship, and the expulsion of atheists! It is against this background that we should view Jefferson's campaign which culminated in the enactment of the Statute for Religious Freedom of 1786.

Mons. Marbois's Query 17 provided Jefferson with the opportunity to rehearse the story of his own assault on the Established Church and to elaborate on the philosophy not only of religious freedom, but of the "illimitible" freedom of the mind in every area. It is one of the most illuminating of all the passages of the *Notes.*

We can dispose of the history summarily. George Mason's Bill of Rights had asserted that "all men are equally entitled to the free exercise of religion according to the dictates of conscience," but it was another three years before the Anglican Church was legally disestablished. In his Revisal of the Laws, Jefferson had already prepared a bill calling for the complete equality of all churches, and the divorce of Church and State. When Jefferson wrote the *Notes*, the fate of that bill was still uncertain, and he seized the opportunity to make his answer to the Query "on The Different Religions Received in the State," an eloquent plea for religious, and all other, freedom. When, a few years later, the *Notes* were published in London, the bill had triumphantly weathered all opposition and become law, and Jefferson could include it as an appendix in the *Notes*. "The error"—so runs Jefferson's reply to Query 17—

> seems not sufficiently eradicated, that the operations of the mind as well as the acts of the body, are subject to the coercion of the laws. But our rulers can have no authority over such natural rights, only as we have submitted to them. The rights of conscience we never submitted, we could not submit. We are answerable for them for our God. . . . Reason and free inquiry are the only effectual agents against error. Give a loose to them, they will support the true religion by bringing every false one to their tribunal, to the test of their investigation. They are the natural enemies of error, and of error only.

This was directed to the threat of church authority and religious superstition. Jefferson was not, however, content with this; after all there was little likelihood of either in America. To Jefferson the issue was broader: it was the fundamental issue of freedom of the mind from authority of any kind. His argument can stand with *Areopagitica:*

Reason and experiment have been indulged, and error has fled before them. It is error alone which needs the support of government. Truth can stand by itself. Subject opinion to coercion whom will you make your inquisitors? Fallible men, men governed by bad passions, by private as well as public reasons. And why subject it to coercion? To produce uniformity. But is uniformity desirable? No more than of face and stature. Reason and persuasion are the only practicable instruments. To make way for these, free inquiry must be indulged, and how can we wish others to indulge in it while we refuse it ourselves?

Nothing that he ever did gave Jefferson greater satisfaction than this Act which, as Madison assured him—somewhat optimistically—"extinguished forever the ambitious hope of making laws for the human mind," and he included it in his epitaph as one of the three achievements for which he wished to be remembered. Nothing that he ever wrote brought him greater acclaim, in his own lifetime, than the preamble to the Act—not even the Declaration of Independence; it was, as he wrote, "received with infinite approbation in Europe, and propagated with enthusiasm. . . . It is comfortable (he continued, with transparent gratification) to see the standard of Reason at length erected, after so many ages, during which the human mind has been held in vassalage by kings, priests and nobles, and it is honorable for us to have produced the first legislature who had the courage to declare that the Reason of man may be trusted with the formation of its own opinions."

The tyranny of Kings and of Priests was ostentatious and formidable, but in last analysis rested on a tyranny still more intractable—the tyranny of ignorance. How revealing (and how appropriate) that the third accomplishment which Jefferson thought might entitle him to immortality was one of his contributions to overthrowing that tyranny—the establishment of the

University of Virginia. Important as that was in itself—and no *philosophe* elsewhere in the world had to his credit the complete legal, material, and intellectual creation of a university—its importance is symbolic as well as real, for education, which played little part in the Old World Enlightenment, was central to the American. How interesting that to the *philosophes* of the Old World such terms as *Aufklärung, Eclaircissement, Illuminismo*, encompassed the whole of the Enlightenment, but in America enlightenment meant, quite simply, education. And how suggestive that while the Old World made science and scholarship the primary instruments of the Enlightenment, in the New it was rather popular education that was thought to be fundamental.

This was, to be sure, familiar. In Europe education had long been the prerogative of the rich and the well-born. In some of the German states, in parts of Holland, Switzerland, and Sweden, there were changes under way—or gestures toward changes—but almost everywhere it was taken for granted that the vast majority of the people—peasants, workers, servants, soldiers and sailors—would languish in ignorance; such statistics of literacy as we have testify to the triumph of this policy, for over vast areas of Europe not ten percent of the adult population could read or write. The third edition of the Encyclopaedia Britannica justified this philosophy in its article on "Education," which distinguished between the education proper for gentlemen and that suitable for the "lower ranks." "Let the youth who is born to pass his days in this humble station be carefully taught to consider honest, patient industry as one of the first of virtues," it argued. "Teach him contentment with his lot by letting him know that wealth and honor seldom confer superior happiness." Nor did the *philosophes* challenge this view. Urging Frederick the Great to extirpate "the infamous superstition" of orthodox Christianity, Voltaire added that "I do not say among the rabble, who are not worthy of being enlightened, and who are apt for every yoke."

66

And even the gentle Pestalozzi, who was of humble extraction and who all his life identified with the poor and the simple, provided an academic education for the children of the gentry, and a vocational education—two hours of schooling and six hours of work—for the children of the poor.

That made the point, and that was why America required a very different educational philosophy from that which obtained everywhere in the Old World. For there was no "rabble in America," "apt for every yoke," except the unfortunate blacks—quite an exception, that. In America all citizens were expected to be apt for self-government, apt for freedom, apt for progress, apt for happiness. In part because the European class system was not transferred to America, in part because a new society in a new land desperately needed whatever talent was available to meet the challenges which confronted it, in part because the success of self-government depended so palpably on the intelligence and virtue of the people, education speedily assumed a central place in American thought and society. In the seventeenth century education at all levels was permeated with religion and largely managed by the clergy; by the time of the Revolution education had begun to usurp the place of religion and was on the way to becoming the national religion.

This development was implicit in the thinking and explicit in the public conduct of most of the American *philosophes*. Well they knew that the experiment in self-government would work only if conducted by a people intelligent, well-informed, and reasonable, for—as Madison put it—"a popular government without popular information or the means of acquiring it is but a prologue to a farce or a tragedy." They realized, too, that they were constructing political mechanisms of unprecedented complexity and one whose operation required a degree of sophistication which no previous political system had called for. They looked to education to provide the moral foundation for an enduring political system, ameliorate religious antipathies, bridge racial and class misunderstandings, give reality to the principle of equality, justify the logic of freedom, and provide the common denominators of national unity. They depended on it to vindicate the new principle of progress—progress as lifting the general well-being of men rather than as enhancing the culture of an elite. No one put this better than Jefferson in a letter to his old teacher, Chancellor Wythe, written from Paris in 1786:

> If all the sovereigns of Europe were to set themselves to work, to emancipate the minds of their subjects from their present ignorance and prejudices, and that, as zealously as they now endeavor the contrary, a thousand years would not place them on that high ground, on which our common people are now setting out. . . . I think by far the most important bill in our whole code, is that for the diffusion of knowledge among the people. No other sure foundation can be devised, for the preservation of freedom and happiness. If anybody thinks that kings, nobles, or priests are good conservators of the public happiness, send him here. It is the best school in the universe to cure him of that folly. . . . Preach, my dear sir, a crusade against ignorance; establish and improve the law for educating the common people.

"A crusade against ignorance"! That was the crusade upon which so many of the Founding Fathers embarked with all the boldness of Jason seeking the Golden Fleece, and none more boldly or more hopefully than Jefferson. "I have sworn upon the altar of God eternal hostility against every form of tyranny over the mind of man," he had written to his friend Dr. Rush, in 1800, and he kept his vow to the end. . . . "Enlighten the people generally, and tyranny and oppression of body and mind will vanish like spirits at the dawn of day," he wrote when he was already in his seventies, and toward the close of his life he confessed that he still looked "to the diffusion of light and education as the resource most to be relied on for ameliorating the condition, promoting the virtue, and advancing the happiness of man." He had launched his own crusade against ignorance as early as 1779 when he introduced his three-part plan "to diffuse knowledge more generally through the mass of the people": a system of elementary schools (to be maintained at local expense) in every ward of the state, feeding into grammar schools, and eventually into a university; a sweeping reform of the almost moribund College of William and Mary including new chairs of law, medicine, and modern languages; and the creation of a state library. None of this materialized at the time, but Mr. Jefferson was tenacious. He never did get a system of public education which was to bring Virginia abreast with Massachusetts and Connecticut, but what he got was, in the end, more important. He was chairman of the committee which drafted the Land Ordinance of 1785 with its enlightened provisions establishing the policy of setting aside public lands for the support of schools and universities, a policy extended, eventually, to all the territories acquired by the United States. In 1816 he drew up plans for ward schools in Virginia, and the following year launched another and more ambitious plan for general education which included the astonishing provision of a literacy test for citizenship—a provision all the more astonishing in that it was drawn from the proposed constitution for Spain!

The Virginia Assembly did not accept Jefferson's far-sighted proposal for the creation of a state library, but here once again Jefferson had his way. As President of the United States he was responsible for the creation of the Library of Congress, and that responsibility became a very personal one when his own private library—one of the best in the country—provided the basis for what was eventually to be the largest and richest of all national libraries.

Jefferson did not succeed in reforming the College of William and Mary—even his plan to bring over the faculty of the University of Geneva failed—but for a quarter-century he labored to create a university which would hold its own with the most eminent in the Old World and—unlike these—be a bastion of freedom too. When in 1825 the University of Virginia at Charlottesville opened its doors to its first class of students, it was, more than any other institution of its kind in history, the lengthened shadow of one man. It was Jefferson who had drawn up the charter and steered it through the legislature; Jefferson who was chairman of the Board of Trustees, and the first Rector of the University. It was Jefferson who designed every building, every column, every window, every door, every mantelpiece; planted every tree and shrub and flower, laid out every path and built every wall; Jefferson who provided the library, chose the professors and the students, too, and drew up the curriculum. And it was Jefferson who dedicated the institution "to the illimitable freedom of the human mind." Not bad that, for a man in his eighties! The university was, at its birth, not only "the most eminent in the United States" as Jefferson said, but the most enlightened and the most liberal, the most nearly like some of the great universities of the Old World.

All in all it was a record of educational achievement which no other American has ever equaled. If Jefferson was not—like Rousseau or Pestalozzi or Grundtvig—an original educational thinker, he was, with Lord Brougham and Wilhelm von Humboldt, the greatest educational statesman of his day.

In education, as in religion, we see once again the familiar pattern of the New World institutionalization of Old World theories. In France, Germany, and the Italian states ideas boiled to the surface, then subsided and cooled off; in America—and perhaps only in America—they boiled over and enriched the soil around them. It would be mistaken, however, to suppose that

Americans added nothing to the arsenal of Enlightenment ideas. What they added was to be found not in formal philosophy but in an almost instinctive response to the familiar circumstances and needs of American life. It was not that revolutionary ideas from abroad challenged American complacency; it was rather that the revolutionary conditions of American society and economy forced American thinkers to come up with new ideas and new mechanisms. Jeffersonian solutions to problems of religion and education illustrate the working of this principle. The crusade against the Infamy and against Ignorance originated in Europe, but the American contribution was not confined to translating the ideas of a Voltaire about the Church or a Filangieri about education—none of which were really relevant to the circumstances of American life—but to formulating and institutionalizing responses that were relevant. To the crusade against religious establishments and fanaticism Jefferson, for example, contributed the idea of the complete separation of Church and State—something not wholly accepted in the Old World two centuries later. To the crusade against ignorance he added the secularization of education (no European University was secular in the sense that the University of Virginia was), and a democratization of education that carried past the elementary school into higher education.

As he looked about him from his eagle nest at Monticello, Jefferson had grounds for confidence, and even for gratification. His second administration had gone badly, to be sure. Yet Jefferson knew that never before had man been vouchsafed so favorable an opportunity to achieve the good life as he was now, and for the indefinite future, in America—still, "kindly separated by Nature from the exterminating havoc of one quarter of the globe, and too high minded to endure the degradations of the others." Everywhere, so Jefferson believed, the auspices were favorable. Nature was not only abundant but beneficent; and where it was not, science stood ready to improve it. Government was benign, and society flourished in freedom as it could not under tyranny, and flourished in peace as it could not in war. Learning and science, now to be the universal possession of the people, could be counted on to teach wisdom and advance happiness. In such a country, with such a society, under such a government, the lessons of the past were irrelevant, and all that could be hoped for the future of man might come to pass. That was a characteristic Enlightenment faith, but even as Jefferson's accession to the Presidency dramatized the triumph of the Enlightenment in the New World by the choice of a Philosopher as King, the dark clouds of reaction were sweeping across the skies of the Old World. By now most of the ardent hopes of the French Revolution had been betrayed, and though Jefferson still explained that gigantic upheaval as "infuriated man seeking through blood and slaughter his long lost liberties," it was pretty clear that Napoleon had other purposes in mind. Britain was in the throes of a black reaction which would not loosen its grip until after the massacre at Peterloo; the Papacy had recovered much of its former power, the Inquisition returned to Spain, and the Jesuits were given a new lease on life. The Empress Catherine sweeps away all the busts of Voltaire and Diderot, and puts all her pet *philosophes* in jail or ships them off to Siberia, and her successor, Paul, dismantles what is left of the Russian Enlightenment. Karl Theodore expels Count Rumford from Bavaria; in Tuscany, Milan, and Naples the reformers are in disgrace or in chains, and the Venetian Republic is no more, while in Vienna the reforms of Joseph and Leopold have gone by the board. Only America is free from reaction: the priests declaim and the Federalists bluster, but it is Jefferson who is in the new White House, and whose disciples will keep the faith for another quarter century.

For Jefferson had lost none of his faith in those truths which he had once called self-evident. Well might he rejoice that the

Enlightenment, driven out of the Old World, had found refuge in the New, and that Providence had placed him in a position where he might vindicate all its claims: the claims of freedom, the claims of Reason and of the cultivation of Reason through science and education, the claims of agrarian democracy, the claims of peace and of the supremacy of the civil over the military authority; the spacious claims of the commonwealth of Law and the commonwealth of Learning. In the Old World the *philosophes* had advanced such claims but had been wholly unable to realize them, for the kings, who did have the power to vindicate them, had not the will. In America alone the idea and the act could be one, as in America alone the philosopher and the king were one —more triumphantly in Jefferson than in any other figure in the history of the Enlightenment.

Certainly Jefferson's commitment to the Enlightenment was tenacious and unqualified. What he said, at the dawn of his career in Philadelphia and Virginia, he said and did at high noon as Secretary of State and Vice President and President, and in retirement at Monticello as the evening shadows fell. The faith he declared, the convictions he professed, the hopes he nourished, lived on as ardently in the quarter century after his election to the Presidency as in the quarter century before. No other Enlightenment figure on either side of the Atlantic was as consistent, as active, or as effective: not Tom Paine who, after his imprisonment in France, declined into ineffectiveness, not Bentham who increasingly took refuge in his own private world, not Miranda who laid waste his powers in military and amorous adventures, not Lafayette who never really understood the intellectual implications of the Enlightenment, not Goethe whose commitment to the Enlightenment was always ambiguous. Jefferson alone of the great galaxy of the *philosophes* embraced the whole of Enlightenment philosophy, interpreted it with matchless eloquence, added to it from his own well-stored mind, and translated it into law and practice on one of the great theaters of history. Alone of them he kept his faith and played his part well into the new century: perhaps that was merely because he lived long after most of his associates had gone to such heavens as their philosophy permitted them to enter. Let us take leave of him now. It is 24 June 1826. He is eighty-three years old, and feeble, and he has only a fortnight to live, but his mind is still clear and his spirit undaunted. He is explaining to Mayor Weightman of Washington why he cannot participate in the celebration of the fiftieth anniversary of the Declaration of Independence, and making a reaffirmation of the faith of the great Declaration which has sustained him to the end:

> May it be to the world what I believe it will be, the signal of arousing men to burst the chains under which monkish ignorance and superstition had persuaded them to bind themselves, and to assume the blessings and security of self-government. That form which we have substituted, restores the free right to the unbounded exercise of reason and freedom of opinion. All eyes are opened, or opening, to the rights of man. The general spread of the light of science has already laid open to every view the palpable truth that the mass of mankind has not been born with saddles on their backs, nor a favored few booted and spurred, ready to ride them legitimately by the grace of God. These are grounds of hope for others. For ourselves let the annual return of this day forever refresh our recollections of these rights, and an undiminished devotion to them.

3

THE

DECLARATION

OF

INDEPENDENCE:

AN EXPRESSION OF

THE AMERICAN MIND

O<small>N</small> 26 May 1776, that indefatigable correspondent, John Adams, who represented Massachusetts at the second Continental Congress, wrote exultantly to his friend James Warren that "every post and every day rolls in upon us independence like a torrent." Well might he rejoice, for this was what he and his cousin Samuel and his new friend Thomas Jefferson had hoped and worked for almost since the Congress had convened in May of the previous year, this ralliance of public opinion to the cause of independence. It helped, to be sure, that the fatuous George III had proclaimed the colonies in rebellion, and thus encouraged the Americans to take him at his word. But the turning point, certainly in public opinion, had come with the publication, in January 1776, of the sensational *Common Sense*, from the pen of Thomas Paine, the most gifted political propagandist in modern history. And as if to vindicate Paine's aphorism that it was ridiculous for a continent to belong to an island, Washington proceeded to drive General Howe out of Boston, thus demonstrating that Americans need not stand on the defensive, but could vindicate themselves in military strategy quite as well as in political.

All that spring the political current flowed toward independence. In February the Congress had taken the ominous step of authorizing privateers; in March it ventured into diplomatic independence by sending the hapless Silas Deane to France to negotiate for aid; in April it declared economic independence by opening its ports to the trade of all nations—except Britain. No less impetuous was the radical change of sentiment in the states. As early as 26 March, South Carolina adopted a constitution which by implication repudiated the royal connection. Early the next month her sister state to the north instructed her delegates to the Congress to support independence, and in May Rhode Island followed suit. Now Massachusetts and Virginia, from the beginning the leaders in organizing resistance to Britain, took action that proved decisive. On 10 May the Provisional Congress of Massachusetts voted to sound out the towns on the question of independence, and the towns declared that they were ready. Virginia did not lag behind. On 15 May a convention met at the historic Raleigh Tavern in Williamsburg and voted unanimously to call upon Congress to declare for independence. On the very day of the Virginia resolution, the Congress took the fateful step of voting that "every kind of authority under the Crown should be totally suppressed," and recommended that the states set up independent governments.

Now the stage was set for the historic event. On 7 June, Richard Henry Lee of Virginia—"the Cicero of America"—introduced three resolutions calling for independence, foreign alliances, and confederation. The radicals wanted unanimity, and voted to postpone the final vote for three weeks, thus allowing time for debate, and for the hesitant and the fainthearted to come over—or step out. Meantime Congress appointed a committee to prepare "a declaration of independence": Dr. Franklin, John Adams, Roger Sherman, Robert Livingston, and, the youngest of all, Thomas Jefferson.

Jefferson had come up to the Continental Congress the previous year bringing with him "a reputation for literature, science and a happy talent of composition." His writings, said John Adams, who rarely had any good to say of others, "were remarkable for the peculiar felicity of expression." Back to Virginia in December 1775, Jefferson had not found it possible to return to the Congress until mid-May of the next spring, just in time to achieve immortality. In part because of that "peculiar felicity of expression," in part because he already had a reputation of working with dispatch, in part because it was thought that Virginia, as the oldest, the largest, and the most deeply committed of the states should take the lead, the committee unanimously turned to Jefferson to prepare a draft declaration. We know a good deal about the composition of that draft: that Jefferson wrote it standing up at his desk (still preserved) in the second-floor parlor of a young German bricklayer named Graff and that he completed it in two weeks. We have his word for it (which is not quite the same as knowing) that he "turned neither to book nor pamphlet" and that all the authority of the Declaration "rests on the harmonizing sentiments of the day, whether expressed in conversation, in letters, printed essays, or in the elementary books of public right, as Aristotle, Cicero, Locke, Sidney, etc." We know, too, that the body of the Declaration—that long and depressing catalog of the train of abuses and usurpations "designed to reduce the American people under absolute despotism"—was taken over from a parallel list of grievances which Jefferson had included in his draft constitution for Virginia only a few weeks earlier. And we can readily accept Jefferson's statement made fifty years later that the object of the Declaration was "an appeal to the tribunal of the world"—that "decent respect to the opinions of Mankind" invoked in the Declaration itself; certainly it was

not to find out new principles, or new arguments, never before thought of; not merely to say things which had never been said

79

before; but to place before mankind the common sense of the subject, in terms so plain and firm as to command their assent, and to justify ourselves in the independent stand we are compelled to take. Neither aiming at originality of principle or sentiment, nor yet copied from any particular and previous writing, it was intended to be an expression of the American mind, and to give to that expression the proper tone and spirit called for by the occasion.

In the end the Declaration was adopted pretty much as Jefferson had written it. There were, to be sure, a good many verbal changes—some twenty altogether (mostly improvements)—and Jefferson was persuaded to add three short paragraphs to his original text. The most grievous change, in his eyes, was the elimination of what John Adams called his "vehement philippic" against Negro slavery and the slave trade—one of the earliest expressions of Jefferson's lifelong detestation of the "peculiar institution." In some ways it was well that that paragraph dropped out, for in a curious way it struck a false note: it was rhetorical without being passionate, and it was bad history. Alas, these were not the reasons why it was eliminated, but rather the reluctance of southern delegates to endorse so extreme an attack upon slavery.

After almost three days of debate Congress adopted the Declaration of Independence, though New York still refrained from voting. Jefferson remembered later that on the 4th of July "the Declaration was signed by every member present except Mr Dickinson," and that legend has entered American history and art: witness the famous John Trumbull painting now hanging in the Library of Congress. Actually, however, it was not until 19 July that Congress provided that the Declaration be engrossed on parchment, and it was on 2 August that the document, "being engrossed and compared at the table" with Jefferson's original, was signed by all the members present.

Interestingly enough it is not Jefferson, but the more passionate and volatile John Adams, who has left us the most moving commentary on the events of this week when the declaration was proposed, debated, and voted:

> You will think me transported with enthusiasm [he wrote to his wife Abigail], but I am not. I am well aware of the toil and blood, and treasure that it will cost us to maintain this declaration and support and defend these states. Yet through all the gloom I can see the rays of ravishing light and glory. I can see that the end is more than worth all the means, and that posterity will triumph in that day's transaction, even although we should rue it, which I trust in God we shall not.

When Jefferson wrote that the Declaration was "an expression of the American mind," what he referred to was almost certainly the Preamble. That Preamble was an expression of more than the American mind; it was an expression of the mind of the Enlightenment. It was because Jefferson was so broadly cosmopolitan that he could sum up the thinking of the Enlightenment in the realm of political philosophy, and because he was so authentically American that he could transform that philosophy into American principles and realize it in American institutions.

Nothing is more fascinating than this Preamble, which summed up with matchless lucidity, logic, and eloquence the philosophy which presided over the argument for the Revolution, the creation of a new political system, and the vindication of the rights of man—and all in less than two hundred words! It is here that we best find the expression of what is universal rather than parochial, what is permanent rather than transient, in the American Revolution. For where most of the body of the Declaration was retrospective, the Preamble was prospective: in the years to come it would be translated into the basic institutions of the American Republic, and not of the American alone.

Consider the opening words of the Declaration: "When, in the course of human events . . ." That places the Declaration, and the Revolution, at once in the appropriate setting, against the background not merely of American or of British but of universal history; that connects it with the experience of men everywhere, not at a moment of history, but in every era. This concept of the place of America in history is underlined by successive phrases of that great opening sentence. Thus the new nation is to assume its place "among the powers of the earth"; it is not the laws of the British Empire, or even of history, but of "Nature and Nature's God" which entitle Americans to an equal station; and it is "a decent respect to the opinions of *mankind*" that requires this justification. No other political document of the eighteenth century proclaimed so broad a purpose; no political document of our own day associates the United States so boldly with universal history and the cosmic system.

Turn, then, to those principles which Jefferson, serenely confident of their ultimate vindication, called "self-evident truths." That phrase, too, is an expression not only of the American mind, but of the mind of the Enlightenment which Jefferson so admirably represented. We would not today assume a body of "self-evident truths," certainly not in the arena of government or politics. Truths today—even the term is suspect—have to earn their way, as it were, have to submit their credentials to the tests of the laboratory and the computer, and even if they pass these they are regarded with suspicion and confined to strict limits of time and place. But the Enlightenment was confident that the reason of man could penetrate to ultimate truth, and that truth, once discovered (or apprehended), was not only as self-evident as a maxim of Euclid, but was both permanent and universal. Nor did it acknowledge different orders of truth, one for the lofty realms of mathematics, another for the more earth-bound regions of the flora and the fauna that were the concern of a Linnaeus and a Buffon, and still another for society, politics, and the economy. What applied to the world of physics, that

> Nature and Nature's laws lay hid in Night
> God said, Let Newton be, and all was light

applied equally to the world of politics and of the law. God said (at least in a Popean sense) let Montesquieu be, God said let Blackstone be, God said let Haller be. . . . This was familiar enough in America. Listen to the youthful Franklin:

> How exact and regular is everything in the *natural* World! How wisely in every part contriv'd. We cannot here find the least Defect. Those who have studied the mere animal and vegetable Creation demonstrate that nothing can be more harmonious and beautiful! All the heavenly bodies, the Stars and Planets, are regulated with the utmost Wisdom! And can we suppose less care to be taken in the Order of the Moral than in the natural System?

Jefferson, who had studied the logic, the order, the perfection of the natural world, sought to impose something of that same order and perfection on the social and the political and the moral world: thus his passion for Palladian architecture, for systematizing his vast library, for introducing order into the criminal code of Virginia, for drawing up rules of order for legislative debates, for classifying Indian languages, and for imposing the decimal system on American currency.

Let us return then to the "self-evident truths," and list them as Jefferson presents them:

83

That all men are created equal;

That they are endowed with "unalienable rights";

That these rights include life, liberty, and the pursuit of happiness;

That it is to *secure* these rights that government is instituted among men;

That governments so instituted derive their powers from the consent of the governed;

That when a form of government becomes destructive of these ends, men may alter or abolish it; and

That men have the right, then, to institute new governments designed to effect their safety and happiness.

Now neither Jefferson nor the American people invented these principles. They were drawn from classical literature (with which all educated men of that day were familiar); they were elaborated by the generation of Lilburne, Cromwell, Sidney, Milton, and above all John Locke in seventeenth-century England; they were popularized by the incomparable Cato (really John Trenchard and Thomas Gordon) whose *Letters* kept alive the spirit of the Commonwealthmen; they were an integral part of the assumptions of the Age of Reason; they were—or appeared to be—rooted in American colonial experience. Jefferson's "self-evident truths" were no more original than were the arguments of Tom Paine's *Common Sense;* the Declaration of Independence was itself simply the common sense of the matter. That is one reason why it was so readily and so generally accepted; that was why it was read with rapture in so many parts of the globe. For the Declaration inspired radicals such as Joseph Priestley, and Horne Tooke, and John Cartwright in England, and rebels like Grattan and Fitzgerald in Ireland; it inspired the enthusiasm of those *philosophes* who were the precursors of the French Revolution, such as Mirabeau, Condorcet, Brissot, and Lafayette; it gave comfort to liberals everywhere: Johann Moser and Christoph

Ebeling in Germany, Vittorio Alfieri and Gianrinaldi Carli in Italy, the intrepid Francis van der Kemp in Holland, who found refuge in America, Henrick Steffens in Denmark, and Isaac Iselin in Basel. It fired the spirit of Francisco Miranda, and of many other leaders of the South American crusade for independence, and perhaps freedom. It entered into the mainstream of history, and worked like a ferment all through the nineteenth and twentieth centuries; in 1945 Ho Chi Minh proclaimed the independence of Vietnam with a declaration modeled on that which Thomas Jefferson had written 170 years earlier.

What Americans did was more important than invent new principles; in the telling phrase of John Adams, "they *realized* the theories of the wisest writers." They actualized them, they legalized them, they institutionalized them. That was, and remains, the supreme achievement of the American Revolution; indeed, in the longer perspective, that *was* and *is* the American Revolution.

Thus—if we take up Jefferson's principles one by one—the idea of natural rights was as old as Greek philosophy, and one which had been invoked again and again over the centuries. But it was only in America, for the first time, that it was formalized and written into constitutional guarantees, only then that the notion which had for so long lingered in the realm of the abstract was endowed with life and clothed in the majestic raiment of the law. Thus for over two thousand years philosophers had argued that government is limited; the revolutionary generation went further, and insisted that God himself was bound by his own laws of justice and mercy. All well enough as long as men gave only lip service to this revolutionary idea. But in fact no government ever had been really limited, not voluntarily anyway: the history of government (as Americans read it) had been an unbroken record of tyranny, and every monarch in Europe still exercised tyranny: even George III, particularly George III. When Jefferson wrote that it was "to preserve rights" that gov-

85

ernments were instituted among men, he meant just what he said, and so did those who signed the Declaration: that the function of government was to preserve the unalienable rights of men, and that if government failed in this duty, it forfeited its claim to legitimacy. After all, even before he wrote the Declaration, Jefferson had drawn up a model constitution and bill of rights for Virginia (neither was adopted but some of his suggestions were incorporated into both) and both these documents were designed to limit the power of government with the utmost care. Soon constitution makers were busy in every state of the new nation doing what Jefferson and his associates had done so well in the oldest of American commonwealths.

So, too, with the principle that government is formed by compact, and that governments thus formed *derive* all their power from that compact and are limited by its terms. An old theory, this, one which had bemused philosophers for centuries and had received classic formulation by John Locke in the seventeenth and Jean Jacques Rousseau in the eighteenth centuries. Whether in some remote past men ever had come together to set up government, we do not know; what we do know is that this was the way government originated in America, and the way it continued to originate for two centuries: by the compact in the hold of the tiny *Mayflower*; in those *Fundamental Orders* which the freemen of three frontier towns along the Connecticut drew up in 1639; by the constitution formed by the pioneers of the short-lived Transylvania colony in 1775; by the settlers of early Oregon who in 1843 convened the so-called Wolf conventions, took affairs into their own hands, and drew up the first Organic Law west of the Rockies; by the followers of John Frémont, who in 1846 launched the Bear Flag revolt, and met together to set up a "Republican Government which shall ensure . . . liberty and virtue."

Thus, too, with what now seems a kind of intuitive genius,

Americans solved that most intractable problem: how men make government. They institutionalized the solution in the constitutional convention, a contrivance which has some claim to be the most important political institution of modern times, for it provided the basic mechanisms of democracy. And along with these, it provided a legal way for men to "alter or abolish" governments: to alter by amendments, or to abolish by wiping the slate clean and drawing up a wholly new constitution. Thus, for the first time in history men legalized revolution. As Alexander Hamilton wrote, the Constitutional Convention "substituted the mild influence of the law for the violent and sanguinary agency of the sword." Jefferson put it more elaborately: "Happy for us that when we find our constitution defective and insufficient to secure the happiness of our people, we can assemble with all the coolness of philosophers and set it to rights, while every other nation on earth must have recourse to arms to amend or restore their constitutions."

The implementation of other principles in the Preamble was more difficult if only because they did not lend themselves so readily to institutionalization. What, after all, did Jefferson mean by such terms as "created equal," or "pursuit of happiness?" These are not only difficult questions, they are in a sense unfair questions. No language, as James Madison observed, "is so copious as to supply words and phrases for every complex idea or so correct as not to include many equivocally denoting different ideas."

There is little doubt that Jefferson used, and that his associates in the Congress endorsed, the term "created equal" in a quite literal sense, for that is the sense in which the Enlightenment embraced and applied the term. What Jefferson meant was that in the eyes of nature (and doubtless of God) every child was *born* equal. All subsequent inequalities, those of race, color, sex, class, wealth, even of talents, derived not from nature but from society, or government, or law. Nature, after all, did not decree the inequality of blacks to whites. Nature did not decree the subordination of the female to the male—there was some ground for thinking it might be the other way around. Nature did not impose class distinctions, or political distinctions, or religious distinctions; it was not even certain that nature imposed physical or intellectual distinctions. Give every child an equal chance, from birth, at health, education, and happiness, and who could foresee the result? This was not merely Jefferson's idea when he wrote of the "aristocracy of talent," but one widely held by the *philosophes* whose pervasive principle was that men were everywhere and at all times fundamentally the same. Yet neither the *philosophes* nor the enlightened despots of the Old World made any effort to translate this principle of equality into practice, as did the Americans, Jefferson among them. "I tremble for my country," wrote Jefferson as early as 1782, "when I reflect that God is just; that his justice cannot sleep forever. . . . The Almighty has no attribute which can take side with us." That the Founding Fathers did not succeed is a reflection on their authority, not on their wisdom. After all we of the twentieth century have not succeeded either, yet we do have the authority. What we lack is the will.

"Pursuit of happiness" is a more elusive phrase, yet the idea that God and nature intended that men should be happy was a commonplace of eighteenth-century thought. In the Old World, however, happiness tended to be an elitist concept, something that the privileged few might possibly achieve by cultivating beauty and wisdom and leisure and the social graces: an expensive business, this, and not ordinarily available to the masses of the people. As America had no elite—not, certainly, in the Old World sense of the term—happiness here was presumed to be available to all who were white, and it consisted, not in the enjoyment of art and literature, science and philosophy, and social position, but rather in material comfort, freedom, independence, and access to opportunity. Happiness meant milk for the children, and meat on the table, a well-built house and a well-filled barn, freedom from the tyranny of the state, the superstition of the church, the authority of the military, and the malaise of ignorance. Jefferson, who knew and indulged himself in the Old World forms of happiness, was entirely willing to abandon them—and indeed to banish them from his own country—in favor of the more simple, the more innocent, and the more just happiness which he thought available in his own country. And to the attainment of these, and their preservation, he made not only philosophical contributions but practical contributions as important and as far-reaching as those made by any other man of his time.

4

THE PURSUIT

OF HAPPINESS

In the eighteenth century all the philosophers were moralists, whatever their philosophy, whatever their religion. They were not pious, they were not devout, certainly they were not orthodox, but they had a religion all the same. It was the religion of happiness. That is what they were after in morals, politics, society; that is what they were after in life itself. Not the answer to the old question, What shall I do to be saved, nor the more familiar question, What is man's whole duty to God. No, theirs was a secular religion. What must man do to be happy? What should government do to assure happiness to its citizens? Pope had made this clear, Pope who summed up so neatly what the age thought:

> O Happiness! Our being's end and aim
> good, pleasure, ease, content, whate'er thy name:
> that something still which prompts the eternal sigh
> for which we bear to live, or dare to die.
> *Essay on Man*

For once, Rousseau and Voltaire agreed. "Happiness is the end of every sentient being," said Emile's devoted tutor; "it is the first desire impressed on us by nature, and the only one that never leaves us." And Voltaire said more simply that "happiness is the object, the duty, and the goal of all sensible men." The Abbé Raynal added to this that "there is, properly speaking, only one virtue, which is justice, and only one duty, to make one's self happy. The virtuous man is he who hath the most exact notions of justice and happiness, and whose conduct conforms most rigorously to them"

Was there ever a generation so obsessed with happiness? Everyone talked about it, everyone wrote about it, everyone sought it. Open where you will the theological tracts, the philosophical treatises, the histories, the poems and plays and novels of the time, the story is the same. Like the song of a whippoorwill comes the refrain, felicity, felicity, felicity. The French immersed themselves in it and made a career of it; the English considered it and rationalized it; the Germans analyzed it; the Italians wrote operas about it; in America it was not only Romantics like Jefferson and Tom Paine who invoked it, but sober statesmen like Washington and John Jay and dour statesmen like John Adams. Montesquieu wrote an *Essay on Happiness*, and the learned Muratori down in Modena submitted a comprehensive treatise, *De la Pubblica Felicità:* what he really wanted was what we would call a welfare state. The tough-minded Dr. Johnson made the pursuit of happiness the theme of his only novel. Imprisoned in the Happy Valley, and surrounded by everything that could pander to the senses or gratify the desires, Rasselas, Prince of Abyssinia, is bored and desperate, and thinks only of escape. Accompanied by his philosopher friend Imlac, he makes his escape, and for years searches everywhere for happiness. In vain; no one is really happy, and in the end Rasselas returns, disillusioned, to his prison. That is life—the everlasting search for happiness. Voltaire wrote on happiness, in the *Philosophical Dictionary*, and Helvetius, who consulted him about a theme worthy of his pen, composed a long poem *Le Bonheur*. Johann Friedrich Struensee, who later became prime minister of Denmark, began his career by editing a *Zeitschrift für Nützen und Vergnügen* and his later career made clear that it was the *Vergnügen* that interested him most—poor Struensee, beheaded and quartered because he sought happiness not only for the Danish people, but for himself and his Queen! In Warsaw, the College of Nobles sponsored a series of public lectures on "Man's Happiness Here Below" and there was even a secret society, *l'Ordre de la Félicité*. The Marquis de Chastellux, who was a General to boot, did not agree with Dr. Johnson about the futility of the search for happiness. He provided a two volume history of that search, *De la Félicité* (*On Public Felicity or Considerations on the Lot of Man in the Various Epochs of History* was the English title). No people of the past had ever really known happiness, said the Marquis, not the Greeks nor the Romans, certainly not the hapless victims of the Dark Ages, not even those who lived during the Renaissance—excitement, yes, but not happiness. "But now, at last, we are truly enlightened; now happiness is within our grasp."

Meantime the dramatists and librettists played incessantly with the theme: Goldoni and Carlo Gozzi, and Beaumarchais and Da Ponte who ended up in the New World, not at all happy. And from Misson's *Voyage of François Legant* (1708) and *Robinson Crusoe* (1719) to Sebastian Mercier's novel about *The Year 2440* (1770) and Saint-Pierre's lachrymose *Paul and Virginia* (1787) novelists sought happiness on some island paradise or in some imagined Utopia.

All well enough, but what is happiness? What is it, where is it to be found? "Real happiness," wrote the Marquis d'Argens, "consists first in not having any crime on the conscience; second being able to rest content in the station to which God has called us; third, a clean bill of health." It was poverty, frugality, temperance, courage, wrote the Abbé De Mably, who thought that only a communistic society could nourish these virtues. It was nature, it was the pastoral life, said Rousseau. Not at all, wrote Chastellux, happiness depends on a hundred things: climate, legislation, natural wealth, and it finds expression in lifting the burden from the toilers of the world. It was to live under a philosophical king —perhaps some Chinese Emperor—said Christian Wolff and promptly lost his job for his temerity. It was a divine project, said the mighty Blackstone, who was not usually so abstract; it was the greatest possible abundance of objects for our enjoyment, said Mercier de la Rivière; it was education and improvement, said Joseph Priestley. It was Freedom, it was Enlightenment, it was a flourishing population, said the Americans. From all of which we conclude with Pope:

> Who thus define it, say they more or less,
> than this, that happiness is happiness?

Surely there must be somewhere a common denominator. And so there is. Man was born to be happy, why is he everywhere unhappy? With one voice the philosophers answer, Because government, religion, society, the institutions of civilization prevent it. Turn where you will, you can see how these artificial contrivances frustrate the native goodness and happiness of man. The poor who work from morning to night for a pittance are ground down by taxes and oppression, decimated by disease and death; even their little children are not exempt from the burden of civilization. Incessant wars drain away the young men, and destroy them, while armies ravage the land that nature intended for the bounty of man. The Church tyrannizes over the minds of its victims, keeps them in ignorance, plagues them and robs them, and if they protest they can expect the fate of a Calas or a La Barre. Even the rich and the powerful are unhappy. They are enervated by luxury, plagued by ambition, eaten by envy, poisoned by jealousy. They are condemned to idleness, and waste their talents in senseless debaucheries. They are strangers to the happiness that flows from simple virtue, to the faithfulness of husband or wife, or the affection of children. They are slaves to the King, to the Church, to Society, as truly as the poor blacks stolen from Africa and carried to the Indies. . . . Society was the enemy of happiness. Look at Candide, look at Cunegonde. How touching their search for happiness and how futile, until in the end they learned to cultivate their garden.

Only Man in a state of nature was happy. Man before the fall.

*

Now the Noble Savage stalks into the salons and the courts of Europe in all his naked majesty. He was a South sea islander; he was a Huron or a Cherokee; he was an Inca Emperor before the coming of the wicked Pizarro; he was some child of nature, Paul or Virginia on a wind-swept island of the Indian Ocean; he was a rude Corsican or a Caledonian, or even a Viking. He was anything and everything but a modern European.

He was the Tahitian chief, Orou, who instructed one of Bougainville's young clerics about love and virtue—especially love. Diderot wrote it all down for the edification of those who still clung to the absurd notions of the Church about these matters (*Supplement to Bougainville*). He was Prince Lee Boo of the Pelew Islands, brought over to England by Captain Wilson of the *Antelope*, where he disported himself and died of the smallpox. He was the wonderful Omai who sailed to England with Captain Cook in 1774, and promptly became the darling of the Court and of drawing rooms. Dressed in a suit of Manchester velvet lined with white satin, with lace ruffles at his wrists, he was presented

97

to the King. "How-do King Tosh," he said, and the delighted George III gave him a sword which he thereafter wore. Joseph Banks carried him from one country house to another, and Lady Sandwich conceived a passion for him (it was to her husband that George III addressed the famous letter of condolence on the death of his mistress). Joshua Reynolds painted him in a flowing toga because that is the way he should have looked, and Mr. Dance painted him in his native costume; he dined with Dr. Johnson; Fanny Burney put him in her diary; and a hundred poets wrote verses about him and his island paradise. He proved how civilized savages could be, and went back to his island home with a barrel-organ, a box of muskets, and his sword, and promptly died.

Or turn to the forests of America for your Noble Savage. He was some Indian like John Shebbeare's Cannassatego. "No human form was ever seen more graceful," wrote his biographer, "his person was straight as the arrow which his hands directed from his fatal bow, his stature six feet, the most perfect height in human nature," and "from his eyes flashed forth beams of courage and compassion, as each passion, at different moments, animated his bosom, within which his heart beat with honest throbbing for his country's service" (*Lydia, or Filial Piety*, 1755). Or he was the Noble Adario who conducted that profound philosophical conversation with Lahontan which contrasted so painfully the virtues of savage life with the vices of European. Or perhaps he was the Abbé Lafitau's Huron, indubitably the descendant of Achilles or Agamemnon. Half a century later the romantic Irish rebel, Lord Edward Fitzgerald, discovered that the red men were still nature's noblemen. He had fought on what he came to believe was the wrong side in the American Revolution; he went back to America, was adopted into an Indian tribe in New Brunswick, yearning to cast his lot forever with his forest friends. "Savages," he wrote, "have all the real happiness of life, without any of these inconveniences or ridiculous obstacles to it." If only he were a savage he would never again be plagued by politics, fashions or duties. Poor Lord Edward, so passionate for liberty, killed in the Irish uprising of 1798.

Even the Americans, who should have known better, succumbed to the myth of the Noble Savage. Here was Mrs. Morton's *Ouabi* who possessed:

> Native reason's piercing eye
> melting pity's tender sigh,
> changeless virtue's living flame,
> meet contentment, free from blame
> open friendship's gen'rous care.

And here was Philip Freneau's Creek Indian Tomo-Cheeki (stolen, no doubt, from John Cleland's Tombo-Chiqui of 1758), languishing in a Philadelphia garret, and longing for the life of the forest. "Why," he asks, "hath my countrymen sent me to make a treaty with white men who are corrupt and dishonorable . . . who hath proved proud, cruel, base, and treacherous?"

The Noble Savage did not even have to be a savage, just so he was primitive, just so he was nature's child. Look at Paul and Virginia on their island in the Indian Ocean: "No care had troubled their peace, no intemperance had corrupted their blood, no misplaced passion had depraved their hearts. Love, innocence and piety possessed their souls. Still in the morning of life, they had all its blooming freshness, and surely such, in the garden of Eden, appeared our first parents when coming from the hands of God." This, as no less than Napoleon observed, is the "language of the soul." Or consider the proud Corsican, Paoli, noble leader of a noble cause, a figure out of Plutarch. Rousseau wrote a constitution for him; Boswell adopted him, and Mrs. Macaulay tried to. England almost went to war for him. The Philadelphia painter Henry Bainbridge painted him; the Americans named a town after him—an ill-fated town as it proved. Sometimes the philosophers went back to an earlier day to find the children of nature in their primitive nobility. Every one knew Juba, the Numidian chief, whom Addison had immortalized in his *Cato*. Juba admired the Roman Cato, but were not the Africans even nobler? Listen to Styphas, general of the Numidians:

> Believe me, Prince, there's not an African
> that traverses our vast Numidian desert
> in quest of prey, and lives upon his bow,
> but better practices these boasted virtues. . . .
> *Cato*, Act. i, Scene IV

Perhaps you would prefer the Vikings, whom the enterprising Paul Mallet was restoring to their place in history, a primitive people, but nature's noblemen. Or consider Macpherson's Celtic bard, the incomparable Ossian, or the Barbarians sweeping down from the German forests to overrun—and reinvigorate—Rome. "The giants of the North," wrote the great Gibbon, "restored a manly spirit of freedom, . . . while" the untutored Caledonians, "glowing with the warm virtues of nature," contrasted with "the degenerate Romans polluted with the mean vices of wealth and slavery."

What did they have in common, these children of nature on the little islands of the South Pacific, or in the forests of Canada, or the towering Andes, or the rude mountains of Scotland or along the fiords of Norway? What they had in common was that they were not Europeans, not contemporaries. They had in common the absence of government, laws, churches, and social classes. They had in common the absence of cities, commerce, industry, money to corrupt, wealth to enervate. Their world was the world of nature. Like Tomo-Cheeki they "rose early to hail the first dawn of the sun; they ran amidst the luxuriant vegetation of nature beneath trees bending with plump and joyous fruits; they quaffed their thirst in the clear waters of the streams."

What is more, like the South sea islanders and the Hurons, they loved as their hearts dictated. "Nor do we think less of our young women if before they are married they indulge in that amiable passion," said Tomo-Cheeki. Above all they were uncorrupted by Europe. "It is impossible," says the Old Man to the innocent Paul of *Paul and Virginia*, "for a person educated according to nature to form an idea of the depraved state of society" of that world. "You Europeans," exclaimed Saint-Pierre, "whose minds are imbued from infancy, with prejudices at variance with happiness, cannot imagine all the instruction and pleasure to be derived from nature. Your souls, confined to a small sphere of influence, soon reach the limits of its artificial enjoyments, but nature and the heart are inexhaustible."

Nature—and the heart! But it was not nature unalloyed, nor the heart untutored, and a kind of bright falseness shimmers over it all. Adario displayed the learning of a savant; Omai delighted London with his wit; Tomo-Cheeki was a veritable *philosophe;* Orau confounded the seminarians with his logic; Logan, the Mingo chief, spoke with the eloquence of a Demosthenes; Ossian was a Celtic Homer. But Adario was really the Baron Lahontan as Orau was really Denis Diderot, and Tomo-Cheeki was of course Philip Freneau, and how much of Logan's eloquence was Jefferson is still a matter of dispute. And as for the blind bard Ossian, he proved a fraud, just as Dr. Johnson had predicted. It was nature, but it was more art than nature. If it was not the art of Versailles or Tivoli, neither was it the nature of the Brazilian jungle. In fact it was all very much like Marie Antoinette milking the cows or dressing in a Greek costume, and Fragonard's children playing in the forests; it was very much like the famous "English" gardens with their carefully wrought naturalness, their touches of the Chinese, their calculated surprises.

Where then was happiness? Was it all in the minds of the

philosophers, like those Utopias described in the imaginary voyages that so delighted this century?

Ah, no, things are not that desperate. There was still America.

*

It was America that had most to teach—English America that is. What could you learn, after all, from Tahiti or China or Corsica that would be of any use? There was not really much likelihood that France would go Polynesian or England Chinese. While London tamed Paoli, Paoli did not inflame London! No, what was needed was some evidence that you could have both nature and civilization, both innocence and sophistication. What was needed was some evidence that you could find, or achieve, virtue and happiness without a convulsive escape to the South seas: some evidence that civilization was not incompatible with virtue and happiness. And for a demonstration of that, where do you go except to America—to those English colonies which were now to be the thirteen United States.

Perhaps it all started with Voltaire—Voltaire who took no stock in nature but voted for civilization, and who loved to contrast Chinese sages with European fops. Voltaire was not really interested in America—it is extraordinary how he manages to ignore it in his *Philosophical Dictionary;* and in his histories, too. But he had discovered the Quakers partly for their own sake, and partly because they provided the most dramatic contrast to the Church, and he equated the Quakers with Pennsylvania and Pennsylvania with Franklin, and Franklin with America. Every step of this equation was a bit misleading, but no matter, the total added up all the same: that's the way it was with Voltaire's arithmetic.

Look at the good Quaker as he goes about his business and the business of God, so simple, so upright, so virtuous, so wise and serene, unspoiled by luxury, untempted by avarice, unseduced by power. "William Penn," wrote Voltaire, "could boast of having brought to the world that Golden Age of which men talked so much and which has probably never existed anywhere but in Pennsylvania." And in his *Discourse on Toleration* he wrote of Pennsylvania that "discord, controversy, are unknown in the happy country which the Quakers have founded, and the very name of Philadelphia, which reminds them constantly that all men are brothers, is the example and the shame of peoples who do not yet know tolerance." (It was of this that Franklin observed that "while we sit for our picture to that able painter, it is no small advantage to us that he views us at a favorable distance.") Where Voltaire led, others followed, and soon Pennsylvania was all the rage, a kind of synonym for Utopia.

Here was the true happy valley, not in Abyssinia; here was innocence, not in Tahiti; here was virtue, not in Maupertius. Here was industry and frugality, here was modesty and kindness, here was freedom and justice. Here men were virtuous and women were chaste; they married young and reared large families. Here was abundance, prosperity, and happiness.

"Do you wish to see a virtuous people?" asked the Abbé Coyer: "Go to a great city, the rival of Paris, there is to be found that remarkable group . . . the Quakers." The good Abbé Robin, who had fought with Rochambeau, was even more enthusiastic about Philadelphia. "Paris has good taste, Philadelphia has a taste for the good; Paris is refined, Philadelphia is simple; Paris has good manners, Philadelphia has pure manners; the French are the most sociable, the Pennsylvanians the most honest of men; Paris has excellent police, Philadelphia has none . . . Philadelphia is a city of happiness." And the Abbé Raynal, as if to make amends for all the unkind things he had said of America, in his *History of the Indies*, made an exception of Pennsylvania. "This Republic, without wars, without conquest . . . became a spectacle for the whole universe. Its neighbors, in spite of their Barbarism, were enslaved by the gentleness of its ways and distant peoples, in spite of their corruption, rendered homage to its virtues. All nations rejoiced to see renewed the heroic times of antiquity which the customs and laws of Europe had made to seem like a fable. They saw at last that people could be happy without masters and without priests." And to prove it all, here was the testimony of the American farmer that the wisdom of Lycurgus and Solon never conferred on man one half the blessings and uninterrupted prosperity which Pennsylvanians now possess: "the name of Penn, that simple and illustrious citizen, does more honor to the English nation than those of many of their kings," he wrote in the second of his letters.

Pennsylvania caught the imagination of Europe, and came to stand for the whole of America.* For Pennsylvania had produced the divine Benjamin Franklin. Fortunate nation, to be the mother of Franklin! He was a child of nature, he was a Philosopher, he was a Quaker, he was a Deist; he was a Wit, he was a Statesman; he was a Scholar, he was a Scientist. He was Solon and Lycurgus, Priam and Ulysses; Condorcet said he was Socrates; he was even Rousseau and Voltaire. With his long white locks falling about his benign countenance, his beaver hat which spoke of the backwoods, his brown homespun suit—on a famous occasion brown velvet—his gold rimmed spectacles of his own make. He was the very picture of innocence and symbol of wisdom. This printer's apprentice from frontier America (for all America was Frontier), had wrested the lightning from the skies and the

---

*Pennsylvania had no monopoly on felicity. Connecticut commanded respect, and so too Virginia. Gaspard de Beaurieu dedicated his *Elève de la Nature* (Nature's Pupil) to the Inhabitants of Virginia. "In that land," he wrote somewhat wildly, "there are to be found neither cities nor luxuries, nor crimes, nor infirmities. Every day of your lives is serene, for the purity of your souls is communicated to the skies above you. . . . You are as nature would wish us all to be."

scepter from the hands of tyrants. He went everywhere, he knew everybody, all doors were open to him and all hearts as well. He wrote for all the journals, he sipped chocolate in all the salons, he made love to all the great ladies—that was safe enough for both sides. He was *Bonhomme Richard* and gave his name to the most famous of ships, ever-victorious. When he and Voltaire met, at the Academy, all Europe exclaimed in ecstasy that it was the meeting of Solon and Sophocles. Every learned society honored itself by counting him a member, and after the revolutionary war, the Royal Society over in London sent him a gold medal for his services to humanity. Even John Adams who distrusted him and envied him could not ultimately withhold his tribute, though he did manage to withhold it for twenty years after Franklin's death:

> His reputation was more universal than that of Leibnitz or Newton, Frederick or Voltaire, and his character more beloved and esteemed than any or all of them. His name was familiar to government and people, to Kings, Courtiers, Nobility, Clergy and Philosophers, as well as to plebians, to such a degree that there was scarcely a peasant or a citizen, a valet de chambre, coachman, or footman, a lady's chambermaid or a scullion in a kitchen who was not familiar with it, and who did not consider him as a friend to human kind. When they spoke of him, they seemed to think he was to restore the Golden Age.

Surely a people who produced Franklin had found the secret of happiness!

Do the Americans know how fortunate they are?

Indeed they do. For the Americans, too, were concerned with happiness. But they were not obsessed with it. They had no need to be. They did not have to ask themselves why man is everywhere born free and is everywhere in chains, why man is born to be happy but is everywhere miserable. For here men were not in chains—not white men, anyway—nor were they miserable. Americans could take happiness for granted as they took freedom for granted. They did not have to romanticize nature, they knew both nature and the Indian far too well to give way to uncritical sentiment. They did not have to revolt against luxury or vice, for they knew neither.

Happiness runs like a golden thread through the thinking and the writing of the revolutionary generation. Their idea of Happiness was almost wholly secular. It had not always been thus. When President Willard of Harvard College, preaching in Boston's Old South Church in 1724, said that "the object of man's happiness is out of himself. Man cannot be his own felicity. . . . The whole creation affords no such object, the fruition whereof can make a man happy. . . . God, and he only, is such an object in the enjoyment of whom there is perfect satisfaction and blessedness," almost all who heard him would have nodded assent. But a generation later, Dr. Samuel Johnson of King's College propounded a very different philosophy, and now we can already detect the influence of Pope or of those philosophers whom Pope reflected, Soame Jenyns, Joseph Butler and Lord Shaftesbury. Here is the Good Angel Raphael, explaining the purpose of God with man. Everything was designed for the pleasure, the happiness, the improvement, and the ultimate salvation of man. Everything, he said, is contrived for the service, the use and benefit of man, the chief and Lord of all.

> How exquisitely is the whole system of nature about you, fitted to every one of your necessities, occasions, and conveniences! How agreeably is your sight feasted with the variety of colors, your hearing with pleasing sounds, your smelling with grateful odors, and your taste with delicious

morsels. In short how exactly is everything fitted to all the purposes both of your subsidence, comfort and delight. And lastly what a wonderful machine is that which you carry about you by which you are enabled to have commerce one with another. (*Raphael or the Genius of English America*)

Happiness, then, is the will of nature and of God. Clearly it is a duty of government and a right of man. The *Pennsylvania Farmer*, John Dickinson, had made this clear as early as 1766: "Kings or Parliaments could not give the rights essential to happiness. . . . They are not annexed to us by parchments and seals. They are created in us by the decrees of providence. . . . It would be an insult on the Divine Majesty to say that he has given or allowed any man or body of men a right to make me miserable. If no man or body of men has such a right, I have a right to be happy." John Adams was no sentimentalist but he wrote in 1776:

> Upon this point all speculative politicians will agree that the happiness of society is the end of Government, as all divines and moral pholosophers will agree that the happiness of the individual is the end of man. From this principle it will follow that the form of government which communicates ease, comfort, security, or in one word, happiness, to the greatest number of persons, and in the greatest degree, is the best.

George Mason, down in his beautiful Gunston Hall in Virginia, picked up the notion from his reading of philosophers, and wrote it into the very first paragraph of the Virginia bill of rights:

> All men are created equally free and independent, and have certain inherent natural rights, of which they cannot, by any compact, deprive or divest their posterity: namely, the enjoyment of life and liberty, with the means . . . of pursuing and obtaining happiness and safety.

107

Jefferson did not go quite that far—but he went to immortality. "Life, Liberty, and the Pursuit of Happiness" was the way he put it, and left it to future generations to quarrel over the meaning of the words. As Robert Frost said in "The Black Cottage,"

> That's a hard mystery of Jefferson's.
> What did he mean? Of course the easy way
> is to decide it simply isn't true.
> It may not be. I heard a fellow say so.
> But never mind, the Welshman got it planted
> where it will trouble us a thousand years.
> Each age will have to reconsider it.

Jefferson returned to this theme again and again—to no one of that generation was it more vital—in his letters and in official statements alike. To General Kosciusko he wrote that "the freedom and happiness of man . . . are the sole objects of all legitimate government." The famous first inaugural address invokes the blessings of "an over-ruling providence which by all its dispensations proves that it delights in the happiness of man here and his greater happiness hereafter"

Tom Paine, too, looked with rapture upon the paradisiacal scene which was spread before the American people at the close of the revolution. Thus, the final number of the *Crisis:*

> Never had a country so many openings to happiness as this. Her setting out in life, like the rising of a fair morning, was unclouded and promising. Her cause was good, her principles just and liberal, her temper serene and firm, her conduct regulated by the nicest steps, and everything about her wore the mark of Honor. It is not every country that can boast so fair an origin.

And more ravishing still was the prospect before Americans:

> To see it in our power to make a world happy—to teach mankind the art of being so—to exhibit on the theatre of the universe a character hitherto unknown.

Nowhere in American literature is there a more touching appeal for the vindication of happiness than in the words of Washington's Circular Letter of 1783:

> The citizens of America . . . are, from this period, to be considered as the actors on a most conspicuous theatre, which seems to be peculiarly designated by providence for the display of human greatness and felicity. Here, they are not only surrounded with every thing which can contribute to the completion of private and domestic enjoyment, but heaven has crowned all its other blessings, by giving a fairer opportunity for political happiness than any other nation has ever been favored with. . . . The foundation of our empire was not laid in the gloomy age of ignorance and superstition, but at an epocha when the rights of mankind were better understood and more clearly defined, than at any former period; the researches of the human mind, after social happiness, have been carried to a greater extent, the treasures of knowledge, acquired by the labours of philosophers, sages and legislatures through a long succession of years, are laid open for our use, and their collective wisdom may be happily applied in the establishment of our forms of government; the free cultivation of letters, the unbounded extensions of commerce, the progressive refinement of manners, the growing liberality of sentiment, and above all, the pure and benign light of revelation, have had a meliorating influence on mankind and increased the blessings of society. At this auspicious period, the United States came into existence as a nation, and if their citizens should not be completely free and happy, the fault will be entirely their own.

And note that Washington returned again and again to this same theme in his Farewell Address.

Meantime the right to happiness was becoming official. George Mason had started it with the Virginia bill of rights. Not to be outdone, John Adams wrote happiness into the Massachusetts bill of rights five times, as well. Thereafter the guarantee of happiness spread from constitution to constitution. If the United States Constitution does not invoke the term, that may be because it was clear that happiness was something the states would take care of. And so they did. Altogether, from the Revolution to the beginning of the twentieth century (when Francis Thorpe made his monumental compilation) there were some 120 state constitutions. Howard Mumford Jones has gone faithfully through them all and discovered that about two-thirds of them provide some kind of guarantee of happiness, and that most of these guarantee not only the right to seek it but the right to obtain it as well. In the United States happiness is not merely a moral but a legal right.

*

The Americans did not really explore happiness: it was too familiar. That was left to a Frenchman who had fought with Montcalm, and then settled in frontier New York. Hector St. Jean de Crèvecoeur, he called himself, and his book, *Letters from an American Farmer*. Happiness is the theme. In the wilderness of America, in the abundance and the freedom of the New World, the husbandman can find happiness. Happiness in farming, and hunting, and fishing; happiness in intimacy with a beneficent nature, in watching the birds, in following the bees, in contemplating the changing seasons of the year, and of life. Happiness in cheerful association with neighbors of whatever race or faith or tongue; happiness in wife and children, the wife not doomed to labor in the fields, but bustling about her cheerful kitchen or sitting at her loom, each child a blessing, not, as in the Old World, a burden. Happiness, too, in the avoidance of war (alas, it came, even to Crèvecoeur's paradise), in the absence of an established church, and of religious quarrels and wars; and happiness in virtue and freedom.

Crèvecoeur strikes this note at once, and it echoes, like some lovely Mozartian refrain, until the very end, when the chords get jangled by war. "Don't you think, neighbor James," says the minister, who appears just this once, "Don't you think that the mind of a good and enlightened Englishman would be more improved in remarking throughout these provinces the causes which render so many people happy? . . . How we convert huge forests into pleasing fields, and exhibit throughout these thirteen provinces so singular a display of easy subsistence and political felicity." So James is persuaded, and undertakes to write his letters to his great friend in England, letters "setting forth the situation and feeling and pleasures of an American farmer."

"I felt myself happy in my new situation," he writes—let us call him Crèvecoeur, now—"and where is that station which can confer a more substantial system of felicity than that of an American farmer?" Where indeed? In his second letter, Crèvecoeur tells us how he inherited his land (no primogeniture here, no entail, no taxes) and extended it by his industry, and how he raised a family, and prospered. "No wonder that so many Europeans who have never been able to say that such portion of land was theirs, crossed the Atlantic to realize that happiness."

Happiness is the theme, too, of the famous *Letter 3*, where Crèvecoeur tells us what is an American, and gives free scope to "the train of pleasing ideas which this fair spectacle suggests." It is one sustained paean of rapture, it is a kind of song of songs to the beauty of America. Who can fail to adore this country, and to cleave to it: a soil that is rich, land in abundance, a salubrious

III

climate; a government that is benign and laws that are mild; a happy intermixture of nations and peoples; a society that is simple and virtuous, religious toleration, peace and friendship, no armies, no tax gatherers, no great cities with their luxuries and their vices. Everywhere "happiness and prosperity," everywhere "hospitality, kindness, and plenty." "Ours is the most perfect society in the world."

So with the additional letters, on Nantucket, on the Vineyard, on Bartram the botanist. The letter on Nantucket opens with the statement that "the happiness of their people" should be "the primary object of the attention of the most patriotic rulers." And so it is. "How happy are we here, in having fortunately escaped the miseries which attended our fathers; how thankful ought we to be. . . ." Nantucket is a veritable Arcadia—there is something about an island, after all —it seems to have been settled "merely to prove what mankind can do when happily governed." It was "not founded on intrusion, forcible entries, or blood, as so many others have been; it drew its origin from necessity on the one side, and from good will on the other, and ever since, all has been a scene of uninterrupted harmony" *(Letter 10)*. "Here, happily unoppressed by any civil bondage, this society of fishermen and merchants live, without any military establishment, without governors or any masters, but the laws; and their civil code is so light that it is never felt."

The moral is the same almost everywhere (not in Charleston, alas, cursed by slavery), and it is driven home relentlessly. Here, for example, is an imaginary Russian gentleman visiting Quaker Bartram. He begins his letter home with a rhapsody to the good fortune of the new world, and concludes with one of those prophecies already becoming commonplace:

O, America! exclaimed I, thou knowest not as yet the whole extent of thy happiness: the foundation of thy civil polity must lead thee in a few years to a degree of population and power which Europe little thinks of.

It was all familiar enough, this celebration of felicity and fecundity. Yet there were some new ingredients, too, and it is important for us to note them. There was, for example, the assumption of material abundance for all—really for all. We take that for granted, but remember that emigration literature (especially the America Letters) for a hundred years was to exclaim in amazement that Americans ate meat every day, that there was milk enough for the children, that there was white bread on the table. There was the assumption of progress. Philosophers, to be sure, had imagined progress, and even made most detailed blueprints of it. But much of the idea of progress in the Old World was the clearing away of obstacles. It was not so much painting a new picture as cleaning off the grime of centuries and revealing the master's original intention in all its beauty. It was doing away with war and injustice, and misery and poverty, and ignorance and corruption—that is one reason the primitive exercised such a fascination for the philosophers. But Americans did not have the problem of overthrowing the past—they did not have a past to overthrow. They started fresh. They could imagine new institutions and new blessings, and realize them too.

Closely allied with the idea of progress was the idea of universal enlightenment. How odd that the term enlightenment in Europe should refer to a program imagined by philosophers and carried through—or neglected—by despots, while in America it meant popular education. "Enlighten the people generally," said Jefferson, and to his old mentor George Wythe, he wrote that "no other sure foundation can be devised for the preservation of freedom and happiness. . . . Preach a crusade against ignorance; establish and improve the law for educating the common people. Let our countrymen know that the people can protect us against the evils of misgovernment."

All the founding fathers were educators: Franklin who founded an academy and a college, and a philosophical society and a library; Washington who left part of his fortune to found a college and ceaselessly advocated a national university; John Adams who wrote into the Constitution of Massachusetts a provision for a learned academy, and privileges for his own Harvard College, and who lived to see his son installed as Boylston professor of Rhetoric; Noah Webster who devoted his life to raising the standards of popular education; Richard Rush who helped found two colleges, and advocated the education of women; William Johnson who represented Connecticut in the Federal Convention and served as first president of the renamed Columbia College; the Pennsylvania Farmer, John Dickinson, who had the happiness to sponsor a college named after him; George Wythe who was not only Chief Justice of his state but Professor of Law at its college. Greatest of them all was Jefferson, who planned a complete educational system for Virginia, wrote educational provisions into the ordinances governing the West, and built the University of Virginia. . . . Where else in the western world do you find anything like this?

There was another ingredient, not new, to be sure, but new in the special meaning it came to hold for America. To the philosophers happiness and virtue consisted in being true to Nature; consisted, consequently, in not being Europe. Americans accepted the first part of this formula only insofar as they identified themselves and their way of life with Nature—which mostly they did. They embraced the second with uncritical enthusiasm.

*

We are in the presence here of one of the great themes of American history and culture: the theme of New World innocence and Old World corruption. It is too large to explore in all of its ramifications but too important to ignore.

The theme of New World innocence and Old World corruption emerged early and persisted all through the nineteenth century: it is a constant of American literature as of American politics, and if it no longer haunts our literature, it still bedevils our politics and diplomacy. Royal feudal Europe may sail with us, as Walt Whitman wrote, somewhat confusedly, but there is perilous stuff in that cargo. Young Philip Freneau warned against the connection with Europe as early as 1772:

> What are the arts that rise on Europe's plan
> but arts destructive to the bliss of man?
> What are all wars, where'er the marks you trace
> but the sad records of our world's disgrace?
> Reason degraded from her tottering throne,
> and precepts, called divine, observed by none.
> Blest in their distance from that bloody scene,
> why spread the sail to pass the Gulphs between.
> *Discovery*, 1772

Why indeed? Why risk infection in these

> Sweet Sylvan scenes of innocence and ease
> How calm and joyous pass the seasons here!
> No splendid towns or spiry turrets rise
> No lordly palaces—no tyrant Kings
> Enact hard laws to crush fair freedom here,
> No gloomy jails, to shut up wretched men;
> All, all are free!—here God and nature reign;
> Their works unsullied by the hands of men.

For here Paradise anew

> shall flourish, by no second Adam lost.
> No dangerous tree or deathful fruit shall grow,
> No tempting serpent to allure the soul,
> From native innocence. . . .

Freneau, it might be said, was at once unsophisticated and enthusiastic. Franklin was neither, but after a long residence in England he could deprecate the notion of a reconciliation between the Americans and the mother country on moral grounds.

> I have not heard what objections were made to the plan in congress, nor would I make more than this one, that, when I consider the extreme corruption prevalent among all orders of men in this old, rotten state, and the glorious public virtue so predominant in our rising country, I cannot but apprehend more mischief than benefit from a closer Union.

It was a sentiment which was echoed by the *Pennsylvania Gazette* the following year: "Remember the corrupt, putrifed state of that nation [Britain] and the virtuous, sound, healthy state of your own young constitution."

How deeply they were shocked, these American innocents, by the goings-on of Europe. Thus the Rhode Island lawyer, Henry Marchant, hoped that "no son of his might wish to see the blaze of princely power and magnificence, or to be overcurious after what the world calls knowledge and wisdom." For to him there was "scarcely any virtue in an American getting to heaven, so infinitely less are the temptations which lead off to dissipation, vice, and folly." Ebenezer Hazard thought London a "sink of sin," and even the loyalist Samuel Curwen was shocked by "vicious indulgences of every kind," while William Samuel Johnson of Connecticut thought the political morality of Britain beneath contempt. "We that have been used to none but sober, regular, fair, and righteous elections, can hardly form any idea without being upon the spot, of those made here, where none of those principles seem to have any share in the business, but the whole depends upon intrigue, party, interest, and money."

Dr. Benjamin Rush, who had studied in Edinburgh and in London, never ceased to preach the danger of contamination from abroad. "America," he said, "should be greatly happy by erecting a barrier against the corruptions in morals, government and religion, which now pervade all the nations of Europe." And years later he was still advising editors to "avoid filling your paper with anecdotes of British vices and follies—duels, elopements, kept mistresses, suicides, boxing matches," stuff which would "destroy that delicacy . . . which is one of the safeguards of the virtue of a young country." David Humphreys, one of Washington's aides, reflected the views of his beloved commander in his poem *On the Happiness of America:*

> All former Empires rose, the work of guilt,
> On conquest, blood, or usurpation built:
> But we, taught wisdom by their woes and crimes,
> Fraught with their lore, and born to better times;
> Our constitutions form'd on freedom's base,
> Which all the blessings of all lands embrace;
> Embrace Humanity's extended cause,
> A world our Empire, for a world our laws.

And Timothy Dwight, later President of Yale College, admonished Columbia:

> Let the crimes of the east ne'er encrimson thy name
> Be freedom, and science, and virtue thy fame.
> To conquest and slaughter let Europe aspire,
> Whelm nations in blood, and wrap cities in fire,
> Thy heroes the rights of mankind shall defend
> And triumph pursue them and glory attend.

Frontier Georgia threatened to deprive young men who went abroad for their studies of their citizenship. With Jefferson— surely the most cosmopolitan American of his generation— American innocence and Old World corruption was almost an *idée fixe*. He expressed this in the famous letter of 1785 to John Bannister, about the education of his son, Mark.

> Why send an American youth to Europe for education? ... Let us view the disadvantages . . . to enumerate them all would require a volume. I will select a few. If he goes to England, he learns drinking, horse racing, and boxing. These are the peculiarities of English education. The following circum- stances are common to education in that and the other coun- tries of Europe. He acquires a fondness for European luxury and dissipation, and a contempt for the simplicity of his own country: he is fascinated with the privilege of the European aristocrats and sees with abhorrence, the lovely equality which the poor and the rich enjoy in his own country. He contracts a partiality for aristocracy or monarchy, he forms foreign friendships which will never be useful to him . . . He is led, by the strongest of all the human passions, into a spirit for female intrigue, destructive of his own and others' happiness, or a passion for whores, destructive of his health, and in both cases learns to consider fidelity to the marriage bed as an un- gentlemanly practice. . . . It appears to me, then, that an Ameri- can coming to Europe for his education, loses in his knowl- edge, in his morals, in his health, in his habits, and in Happiness.

Thank God—or nature—for the Atlantic Ocean! So Jefferson wrote to George Wythe, in 1786:

> If all the sovereigns of Europe were to set themselves to work to emancipate the minds of their subjects, from their present ignorance and prejudices, and that as zealously as they now endeavor the contrary, a thousand years would not place them

on that high ground on which our common people are now setting out. Ours could not have been so fairly put into the hands of their own common sense, had they not been separated from their parent stock and been kept from contamination, either from them, or the other people of the old world, by the intervention of so wide an ocean.

So he wrote, fifteen years later, to the Earl of Buchan:

I feel real anxiety on the conflict to which imperious circumstances seem to call your attention. And bless the almighty being who, in gathering together the waters under the heavens in one place, divided the dry land of your hemisphere from the dry land of ours.

Another fifteen years and he had developed this sentiment into a policy.

The day is not distant [he wrote to his old friend William Short], when we may formally require a meridian of partition ... which separates the two hemispheres ... and when, during the rage of eternal wars of Europe, the lion and the lamb within our regions shall lie down together in peace. . . . The principles of society there and here are radically different, and I hope no American patriot will ever lose sight of the essential policy of interdicting in the seas and territories of both Americas, the ferocious and sanguinary contests of Europe.

The theme, and the arguments, persisted. Young Edward Everett, newly returned from Germany just as Jefferson was formulating those ideas which were to emerge as Mr. Monroe's doctrine, asked rhetorically:

To Europe's History why each thought confine?
Mark where afar in blameless lustre shine
Columbia's stars. . . .

And James Russell Lowell—it was in his anti-British period—advised his fellow countrymen to

> Forget Europe wholly, your veins throb with blood
> to which the dull current in hers is but mud . . .
> O, my friends, thank your God, if you have one, that he
> twixt the old world and you sets a gulf of a sea . . .

It is the most persistent theme in American literature from Crèvecoeur to Cooper, from Hawthorne's *Marble Faun* to *Daisy Miller* and *Portrait of a Lady*, from *Innocents Abroad* to *The Sun Also Rises*. Something of its complexity and difficulty can be seen in the position of the expatriate. Here Americans maintain a double standard; it is taken for granted not only that the European immigrants to the United States give up their nationality and identify themselves with their adopted country, but that they do so exultantly, and Theodore Roosevelt made substantial political capital by his campaign against hyphenated Americans. But for Americans to give up their nationality and identify themselves with a foreign country is another matter altogether.

Needless to say there are philosophical and psychological implications here which we ignore at our peril. For this concept of New World innocence and Old World corruption encouraged that sense of being a people apart already sufficiently dramatized by nature herself. How characteristic that Jefferson should have combined nature and morality in the first inaugural: "Kindly separated by nature from one quarter of the Globe: too high minded to endure the degradations of the others. . . ." To this day Americans are inclined to think that they are somehow outside the stream of history, that they are somehow exempt from the burden of history. The *philosophes* in general ignored the American experience, and so, for long, did European monarchs and statesmen, and Americans were prepared to accommodate themselves readily enough to that attitude, as if it were a reality. "Are we a peculiar people?" asked Chancellor Kent indignantly in the New York Constitutional Convention of 1820. And the answer was of course, yes, we are. Elsewhere human nature condemned revolution to futility, but not in America: here revolution could be orderly and benign. Elsewhere corruption poisoned the body politic, but not here; America was to be miraculously free from corruption! Elsewhere faction set men at each others' throats, but here faction was tamed into party and parties were benevolent. Elsewhere men of different faiths burned each other at the stake, but here they could live peaceably side by side . . . All well enough, especially as it conveniently left out slavery. But there was more to it than this. Other nations experienced defeat, but it was contrary to nature for America to know defeat. Other nations suffered misfortune, but Americans were exempt from misfortune. Other nations had learned from experience or necessity to accept compromise, but it was unbecoming in Americans to accept compromise. Other nations acknowledge limitations long familiar to them, limitations on power, limitations on will, limitations on fortune, but Americans know that the oceans and the skies belong to them.

Perhaps all this is part of that happiness guaranteed the American people in their constitutions.

5

THE AMERICAN
ENLIGHTENMENT
AND THE
ANCIENT WORLD:
A STUDY IN PARADOX

THE PHILOSOPHY of history has always been closely connected with the uses of history. We might even say that the philosophy is determined by the use: that a people, or their historians, select out of the vast ocean of history what they think useful or relevant at the moment, and interpret it in ways that will profit, or perhaps merely entertain, them.

In a broad way we can distinguish two, perhaps only two, large philosophies of history that have endured for long periods of time and commanded general allegiance in the western world. The first is that which we associate with Dionysius of Halicarnassus and, in modern times, with Bolingbroke: history as philosophy teaching by examples. Of all philosophies of history it is the one that has endured longest and that has exercised the greatest influence on the thought and the imagination of man. The second is what poses as scientific history and which we tend, in our own time, to call technical history: the effort to reconstruct the past as it actually was and, in large part, for the sake not of satisfying some current need but of satisfying some individual or collective curiosity.

With the second of these philosophies we need not concern

ourselves. Its origins were, to be sure, in the eighteenth century —perhaps even earlier in the work of the Bollandists and the Érudites, in Vico down in Naples or the almost forgotten Justus Möser of Osnabrück. But these were unknown in America, and almost unknown in their own societies. No, it was the first, history as philosophy teaching by examples—that dominated the thinking of men in the age of the Enlightenment, in America as in the Old World.

It had, after all, the longest and most respectable lineage: it had the magisterial authority of the greatest of ancient writers; it had the immense advantage of combining morality with art, literature, and philosophy. That the function of history was moral was the conclusion of Thucydides and Plutarch, Tacitus and Livy, and most of their successors until modern times. "What chiefly makes the study of history wholesome and profitable," wrote Livy, "is this, that you behold the reasons for every kind of experience set forth as on a conspicuous monument: for these you may choose for yourself and for your own state to imitate, from these mark for avoidance what is shameful in the conception and shameful in the result." So said Machiavelli—less read in America than in Europe to be sure—"that those who wish to learn the achievement of this end [of virtue and triumph] need not take any more trouble than to put before their eyes the lives of good men." So said Sir Walter Raleigh in his ambitious history of the world, that "the end and scope of history is to teach us by examples of times past, such wisdom as may guide our desires and actions."

The purpose and end of history was to discover those grand moral laws that man should know, and knowing, obey. This was the search that sent the eighteenth-century historians back to the ancient world, and persuaded them to reflect on the rise and fall of empires—one of the favorite themes of Enlightenment history. It was what persuaded them to study the Orient—how they delighted in China and all the lessons that it could teach—in America, even in the islands of the South seas. All particular histories were like tributaries, each one carrying its own sediment of truth, pouring it into the great main stream of history where the historians could dredge it up. "The course of things has always been the same," wrote Bolingbroke. "National virtue and national vice have always produced national happiness and national misery." And the great David Hume added that "Mankind are so much the same that history informs us of nothing new or strange in this particular. Its chief use is only to discover the constant and universal principles of human nature."

No need to elaborate on anything so familiar. Let us simply assert that in the eighteenth century almost every historian and statesman (and in America it was the statesmen who were the historians)—or every one except Vico and Möser and their followers, subscribed to this philosophy. "One cannot remind oneself too often of crimes and disasters," said Voltaire who wrote the best of all books on crimes and disasters in *Candide*, "These, no matter what people say, can be forestalled." The American Founding Fathers agreed with this argument. All of them were immersed in history though not under that rubric. They called their histories *Notes on Virginia*, or *The Federalist Papers*, or *The Rights of Man* instead. They drew on history to justify independence and to guide them along the paths of federalism and to help them create a nation.

If history is philosophy and a storehouse of precedents, what history do you draw on? That was easy enough in the eighteenth century. You draw on the history that everyone knew, you draw on the writers that everyone agreed were the greatest that mankind had yet produced, you draw on the ancient world. Rousseau, who was not so much an Enlightenment figure as a precursor of Romanticism, in this spoke for them all. "It was Plutarch that emancipated him from servitude and taught him the noblest virtues" [he was more sure of this than were his critics]: "Ceaselessly occupied with Rome and Athens," he wrote, "living, one might say, with their great men, . . . I thought myself a Greek or a Roman." And the less known Vauvenargues remembered that even as a boy he had found Plutarch irresistible: "I cried with joy when I read those lives. I never spent a night without talking to Alcibiades, Agesilas, and others. I visited the Roman Forum to harangue with the Gracchi, to defend Cato." Over in the American colonies when John Dickinson published the famous Farmer's Letters, a Boston town meeting voted him thanks for "his Spartan, Roman, British virtue."

European philosophers had a bit more choice than the American. They could, after all, turn back to the medieval chroniclers or to the Renaissance historians. But what do you do if you are American, becoming self-conscious as a separate people and eager to assert your separate identity, engaged in a struggle for independence, creating a nation, and building institutions suitable to that new nation?

There was not in fact, a great deal of choice. Americans could not very well draw upon their own historians for the elementary reason that they had so few. There were pious recorders from John Smith and Bradford and Winthrop to the eighteenth century; there was Thomas Hutchinson, who was not yet available. They were reluctant to draw on England—on Clarendon or Hume, for example, though they were happy enough with "the great Mrs. Macauley" who seemed to approve of everything they were doing. They were almost equally reluctant to draw on contemporary European history: after all one of the major themes of this era was the theme of New World innocence and Old World corruption. The quite conscious, and even self-conscious, rejection of the Old World began with Philip Freneau and Hugh Brackenridge and reached a kind of poetic Götterdämmerung in Joel Barlow's now universally unread *Vision of Columbus*. The principle was much better expressed by statesmen; by Franklin; off and on, by John Adams, never really very consistent; by Jefferson who grasped it most profoundly; by Tom Paine who, in a curious way, was the most American of them all in his repudiation of the Old World. They could not turn to what were even then regarded as the "Dark Ages," for the Enlightenment was persuaded that they were indeed dark, a conviction strengthened by the almost universal antipathy to religious superstition. Romanticism, to be sure, was already infiltrating, and would soon make the Dark Ages not so much dark as picturesque: let us not neglect that wonderful picture which Chastellux gives us of his visit to Monticello (itself a curious mixture of the classical and the romantic) sitting up all night with Thomas Jefferson reciting passages from McPherson's *Ossian*—Ossian fraudulent, to be sure, but not the emotions which he inspired. You could, of course (as Europe did) study China—a nice compromise between rationalism and romanticism. That was one way of criticizing existing institutions, as the great Christian Wolff found to his cost—remember he was dismissed from his professorship at Halle and banished from Prussia on pain of death for asserting that the teachings of Confucius were as elevated as those of Jesus. Mostly China was an indulgence and a delight: Chinese gardens, pagodas, silks, porcelain, furniture (imitation of course), and pavilions: there was one at Sans Souci, one at Nymphenburg, a whole village at Cologne, there was a Chinese bridge even at Gray's Inn outside Philadelphia, and, in a stunning example of Nature imitating Art, the Cherokee Rose (state flower of Georgia today) was imported from China via Scotland in the seventeen-nineties. But Chinese history—that was of no possible value to anyone, certainly not to anyone in America.

What was left was the ancient world. The rediscovery of the ancient world was not an American enterprise (indeed the Americans contributed nothing of importance) but an Enlightenment one. It is a familiar story—the work of Winckelmann, who became librarian to the blind Cardinal Albani and rediscovered the ancient world in art and taught his generation to appreciate the universal in beauty and truth—which meant the Greek; the contribution of great architects from Palladio to Burlington, and the brothers Adam, and of decorators like Flaxman and collectors like Caylus, of artists like Piranesi and Boucher and Mengs and eventually the Philadelphia lad, Benjamin West, of a school of sculptors like Canova and Thorwaldsen and Sergel from farthest North, and scores of lesser figures who haunted the ruins and the ateliers of Rome and of Florence. And there was a new and lively interest in the history of the ancient world, an interest fanned by the immensely popular Charles Rollin (a popularity now so hard to understand), and by the contributions of Montesquieu and Gibbon, both addressing themselves to the same importunate theme of the decline of Rome, and—in a different arena—the archeological and historical forays of "Athenian" Stuart, who was also "Roman" Stuart.

The Enlightenment as a whole looked to the ancient world, studied its history, read its literature, imitated its art and architecture, cultivated its philosophy and, in theory at least, embraced its political principles. This was the education of all who had any education: the churchmen, the artists, the lawyers, and the statesmen. There was nothing remarkable about the American fascination with the ancient world; it would have required explanation had the generation of the Founding Fathers turned their attention elsewhere.

What did the historical and moral world of Greece and Rome have to offer Americans of the eighteenth century, or what did Americans think it had to offer?

It provided them with three different though connected reservoirs; one of antecedent practices and institutions, one of historical events and personalities, and one of moral lessons. The antecedents were doubtless more suggestive than real—republicanism in Rome, federalism in Greece, enlightened colonial relationships, the dangers of simple democracy, the perils of distant wars, political institutions like the Senate or the Consuls. It is difficult to know how serious, or even how useful, these antecedents were. No doubt some of the interest in them was rhetorical, and some of it mere intellectual window-dressing. But the point is that the persuasive rhetoric took *this* form, not any other; that the appealing window-dressing was classical, not, let us say, religious. The Founding Fathers knew the ancient world better, perhaps, than they knew the European or even the British world, better, in all likelihood, than they knew the American outside their own section. But it does not follow that they created a republic, a federal system, a new colonial system, because they had studied Cicero or Polybius or Thucydides. Nor is it clear that they learned to hate tyranny, detest corruption, and avoid luxury from their classical mentors. The man who hated these things most vehemently, Tom Paine, was one of the few who had no classical education, and rarely evoked classical antecedents. And—let us remember—the English statesmen who were, presumably, guilty of the vices of tyranny and corruption, and were certainly creatures of luxury, were themselves children of the classical world, and so too the French, German, and Italian aristocrats and rulers who were guilty of so many offenses against the moral principles of the ancient past.

The second feature of the classical inheritance blended inextricably with the third: familiarity with historical events and personages from the Greek and Roman world. Here was history for ready reference, always with the assurance that your auditors or readers would recognize all of the references, catch all the allusions, nod agreement with every argument, rejoice in every apt quotation. You can see this in that monstrous work of plagiarism and of genius, John Adams's *Defense of the Constitutions;* you can read it in the briefer—and livelier—*Farmer's Letters* of John Dickinson, larded as they are with quotations from Latin and with allusions to ancient history. You can catch something of its pervasive role if you glance through the long lists of theses defended by candidates for the master's degree at colonial colleges, which J. J. Walsh has compiled for us. Better yet you can come to appreciate how much the classics were an integral part of the life of that generation from the wonderful correspondence of John Adams and Jefferson. There was an antecedent for everything, and everything that was happening in the New World had already happened in the ancient. You did not need to subscribe to the theory of the remarkable Père Lafitau that the survivors of the Trojan Wars—Greek and Trojan alike—had somehow sailed to America and peopled this continent, and stamped their habits and their characteristics on the native peoples, to realize that there was a certain symbolic truth in this explanation.

More important—at least so it seems now that the historical and institutional antecedents have slipped away from our consciousness—was the moral impact of the ancient world on the American mind. But why did this not work in the European as in the American world? It did—but for obvious reasons it could not in the Old World have the *consequences* it had in the New. After all every philosopher knew the Platonic ideal of philosophers as kings, and doubtless approved of it, but France did not place Voltaire on the throne, or England David Hume, or Austria Joseph Sonnenfels, and even Goethe was not allowed to sit at table with the Duke of Weimar until he had been properly ennobled. But Americans did make their philosophers kings: John Adams and Jefferson and Madison, one after another.

Who can doubt that consciously or unconsciously—and a good deal of the first if we are to judge by commonplace books and memoirs and letters—Americans adopted the Plutarchian models. It was not merely custom that led them to sign Publius and Fabius and Cincinnatus and Epaminondas or to name their country seats Tusculum, or to build in the style of Palladio and model their public buildings after the Maison Carrée, Graeco-Roman despite its French name . . . Washington belonged in Plutarch, and John Jay and Henry Laurens and George Wythe and Jefferson, too—clearly on the Greek side, rather than the Roman, and even, in a way, those two sturdiest of homespun Americans, Benjamin Franklin (was he not Solon, was he not Lycurgus) and John Adams who, at a great moment in his life, wanted to know whether he was to be considered as one of the two kings of Sparta or one of the two consuls of Rome or—for Adams never could leave well enough alone—one of the two suffetes of Carthage. Perhaps of the major Founding Fathers, only Tom Paine would not have been comfortable in a toga: even Franklin proposed that he be painted in one! Oddly enough there was room even for an Aaron Burr: we may think that he belonged more appropriately in an opera by Da Ponte or Beaumarchais, but he could always be labeled Cataline.

It was the moral world of republican Rome that appealed irresistibly to Americans, and it appealed to them because it was their kind of world. The scorn of luxury and effeminacy, the acceptance of austerity; the preference for the rural life, so sweet to Virgil and to Horace, so sweet to Washington and Jefferson and William Livingstone and John Adams; the eloquence—on the whole Ciceronian rather than Periclean; the devotion to the law; the dedication to public service; the sense of honor and dignity and virtue: all of this was as American as it was Roman. Chastellux caught it—even the Plutarchian tone—in his tribute to Washington: "The idea of a perfect whole . . . Brave without temerity, laborious without ambition, generous without prodigality, noble without pride, virtuous without severity, he seems always to have confined himself within those limits, where the virtues, by cloathing themselves in more lively but changeable colors, may be mistaken for faults."

All very true; yet there are reservations and qualifications. The philosophers of the Old World played an active part in the rediscovery and the recreation of the world of Greece and Rome; the Americans did not. Franklin knew Italy, but it was the Italy of Beccaria and Filangieri and their fellow reformers and scientists; Jefferson brought his vignerons from Italy, and smuggled out rice, and copied Villa Rotunda and Villa Malcontenta; all to the good but scarcely archeological. Perhaps only that lonely and forgotten John Izard Middleton of Charleston who wrote a book on *Grecian Remains in Italy* and is remembered, or forgotten, as the model for the hero of Madame de Stael's *Corinne, or Italia*, made a contribution: poor Middleton who was cast neither for an American nor an Italian, but for the English Lord Nelvil. No, the Americans contributed nothing—no "Athenian" Stuart, no Flaxman, no Robert Adam, no Winckelmann, no Montesquieu, no Gibbon, no Goethe, they were borrowers and exploiters; they used the ancient world as they used history in general, to justify their conduct and to illuminate their character. And they used it too—we tend to forget this or to undervalue it—for pleasure, for consolation, for strength.

In some interesting ways, the American obsession with Greece and Rome was even paradoxical; the paradoxes were never resolved because unconsciously there was, for example, the initial paradox of embracing an historical philosophy which sought to be universal and which was, certainly, cosmopolitan, as a support to or an accompaniment of nationalism. For one of the major virtues of the Graeco-Roman world was that it had come closer to creating institutions and principles of universal significance than had any other civilization; that every society, every age, could draw upon it precisely because it was not particular but universal. This is what Winckelmann insisted upon in his interpretation of ancient art, that it had achieved a universal beauty, by comparison with which all particular beauties were insignificant. The languages were universal, at least among the educated —lectures at most universities were delivered in Latin until the beginning of the eighteenth century and Tomasius was forced out of Leipzig in 1694 because he lectured in German—and so too, of course, the literature and the philosophies. But the new United States was embarked upon an original experiment in Nationalism, which is not universal but the epitome of the particular in politics, and in other realms as well. Lincoln was quite right when he said that our forefathers had brought forth a new nation; he did not point out—and most of us overlook—the interesting fact that the United States was the first new nation to be brought forth, the first to be *created,* and that modern nationalism, particularistic and fragmenting, has one of its roots in American soil.

There is the related paradox of the merging of Classicism and Romanticism. Americans were not the only people to do that: you find it in the Germany of Goethe and Lessing, in the Denmark of Holberg and the Swiss-Danish historian Mallet, in the *Supplement to Bougainville,* in much of Rousseau, and in a midcentury England which boasted Pope's *Essay on Man* and the architecture of the Adam brothers, but also delighted in *Ossian,* invented the English Garden, and lost its heart to that noble savage, Omai.

But—it might be said—Europe *contrived* its Romanticism, in the eighteenth century at least, while in America it came natural. Doubtless it was symbolical that Jefferson placed his Palladian villa, with its Italian name, on the very edge of the most romantic wilderness in America—but where in Virginia could he have placed it that was not romantic? America, certainly, did not need to contrive Romanticism. All very well for Emile to get a full-time tutor to reveal nature to him: every American lad would grow up knowing more about nature than Emile ever learned, just by being himself. No need to contrive "English Gardens"; all of America was a natural garden. No need to imagine Utopias on some distant island—Tahiti, perhaps, or Maupertius, where Paul and Virginia grew into such pure and tender love—the whole of America was a kind of Utopia; even Voltaire, who did not believe in Utopias or in Romanticism either, saw that. No need to conjure up noble savages, like Adario or Omai, though Philip Freneau did with his absurd Tomo-Cheeki, and perhaps Jefferson with Logan's eloquence; Americans already had savages, not very noble but familiar enough and the stuff for romance when they got around to romance, and they did not really have to wait for Irving and Cooper. What is clear is that Americans were far more susceptible to the temptations of Romanticism than were Europeans, but still insisted on cherishing Classicism. The observation attributed to the young Benjamin West when he was shown the Apollo Belvedere, "My God how like a Mohawk Indian," may have been John Galt's invention—we shall never know—but certainly it was appropriate.

Here is a third paradox: the classical world represented order, logic, stability, reason (of course there were elements of irrationality in Greek thought and mythology) and represented too not only the universal, as Winckelmann saw, but the permanent. The great works of art and architecture, of literature, philosophy and history, what were they but timeless? But Americans were not dedicated to the stable, the permanent, the timeless; they were committed to change and revolution. Even as they rejoiced in Aristotle (not in Plato very much) or in Sophocles, Solon, Lycurgus, Aristides, Thucydides, Cicero, Polybius, and Plutarch, they were busy changing everything: the principles of government and the instruments of government; the organization of society; the relations of religion and the state; the system of education;

nature herself, for they would not let nature alone.

There are suggestive illustrations of this paradox of embracing at once the fixed, the orderly, the coherent and the permanent, and at the same time the changing and the disorderly and the pluralistic and the evanescent. Consider for example the political contrivances and the political life of the new nation. The contrivances were (and were designed to be) orderly, and certainly systematic. The very names bear witness to the ancient world— Republic, Federalism, President, Senate, Judiciary, and so forth —and they were designed to embody fixed and permanent principles of politics in constitutions. On the surface all is order, all is balance, all is permanence. It did not quite turn out that way, but that is another story. But alongside or underneath all this was a body of disorderly practices—the almost convulsive play of forces which threatened the equilibrium of the formal political institutions: democracy itself, political parties, the changes imposed upon order by the unwritten constitution—another term for the spontaneous growths in society, growths which took over and transformed all the neat contrivances.

Perhaps the most striking paradox of all was in the use to which the Founding Fathers put history. For here you have, most clearly, two schools of thought, two philosophies, if those terms are not too pompous for what took place. We might call them the Classical and the Progressive, or perhaps the Retrospective and the Prospective interpretations of history. By good luck these are represented by the two most articulate, and most representative, of the Founding Fathers: John Adams and Thomas Jefferson. They agreed on so much, fought shoulder to shoulder in so many campaigns, dedicated their lives, fortunes, and honor to the same ends. But how different they were, and nowhere do the differences emerge more strikingly than in the use to which they put history.

Adams was—the generalization is of course far too simple—

homespun, provincial, irremediably Yankee in interest and temperament, passionately attached to his own town, state, sections, and nation, and ineradicably suspicious of the Old World, of all that smacked of the effete, the polished, the mannered, the luxurious, the grace notes, the extravagant, and the immoral. He was, in short, Roman in his virtues. Jefferson was patrician, cosmopolitan, affluent, passionately devoted to music and the arts, more at home in Paris than anywhere except Monticello, happiest with the literature, arts, gardens, wines, society of the Old World. Imagine Adams asking Philip Mazzei to send four vigneron with the specification that each should play a different musical instrument! Yet of the two it was Adams who clung stubbornly to the moral lessons of the Old World, Jefferson who was prepared to disregard them. It was Adams whose uses were almost wholly retrospective, Jefferson whose uses were prospective.

From the study of history Adams drew the melancholy but inescapable conclusion that if human nature and government were indeed everywhere and always the same, there could be no ground to believe that the American people would escape the fate that had afflicted all others. And to counter the consequences of this conclusion, Adams formulated the principle of checks and balances to frustrate the depravity of man and the inherent corruption of government.

But Jefferson was not prepared to accept the laws of history, worked out on the basis of past experience, as a necessary part of the cosmic system or even as part of the historical process. Human nature was not everywhere and forever the same. It might be in the Old World, but not in the New, not in America. Of the two, Adams was doubtless the more deeply immersed in history, but it was Jefferson who made the original contribution —that history is not exhausted. To put it another way, it was Jefferson who gave a new reading to the philosophy of Progress, one peculiarly adapted to the circumstances and needs of America. And, as so often, even in the political arena, it was Jefferson who won out, Jefferson who imposed his views on the future.

So once again the Americans had it both ways. They drew from the ancient world all the right moral lessons, and the right antecedents and precedents too; they drew the names, the mottoes, even the styles; what did they not owe to the ancient world? But at the same time they emancipated themselves from that world, or at least from the limitations which it threatened to impose upon them. They were the creatures of history, but not the prisoners. They were indebted to history, but they triumphed over it.

6

THE PAST AS AN EXTENSION OF THE PRESENT

I‍f we inquire into the historical philosophy and the historical vision of the generation that founded the Massachusetts Historical Society and its sister institution in Worcester, the American Antiquarian Society—the generation of Jeremy Belknap and Isaiah Thomas—we meet, at the very threshold, what seems to us a paradox. This is the contrast between the formal political and the formal historical writing of the American Enlightenment. The generation that gave us indubitably the most profound and eloquent political treatises of our literature, from the Declaration of Independence and *Common Sense* to the debates in the Federal Convention and the *Federalist Papers*, gave us not a single formal historical work that anyone but a scholar can remember, or an Antiquarian read with pleasure, or either except as an act of piety. Hutchinson's *Massachusetts Bay* is accurate, judicious, and pedestrian but in all fairness we cannot claim Hutchinson after destroying his library and scattering his manuscripts to the winds; Gordon's *American Revolution* is plagiarized from the *Annual Register*; Ebenezer Hazard gave us collections, Noah Webster was a dilettante, Mercy Warren, though occasionally sprightly, was, as John Adams made clear, unreliable; John

Marshall's ponderous five volumes on Washington, much of it cribbed from other books, is universally unread. Something is to be said for Jeremy Belknap's *New Hampshire* and Dr. Ramsay's history of the Revolution and Williamson's *North Carolina*, but it is sobering to reflect how long these have been unobtainable. Of all that generation only the grotesque Parson Weems wrote histories that survive, and everyone acknowledges that he was not really an historian at all and that he belongs to the era of Romanticism, not to the Enlightenment.

Yet no other generation in our history has been so preoccupied, we might say so obsessed, with history as the generation of the Founding Fathers, that generation to which the indefatigable Isaiah Thomas indubitably belonged, and none, it is safe to say, wrote better history. For the great historical writings of this generation, we turn to John Adams, Franklin, Paine, Jefferson, Hamilton, Washington, Madison, Wilson, Rush, and their associates among the Argonauts; and the great historical treatises are not formal histories but such works as *The Defense of the Constitutions, Notes on Virginia, The Rights of Man, The Federalist Papers,* James Wilson's *Lectures on the Constitution,* and similar statements.

Turn where you will in the writings of the statesmen and you are launched on the seas of history—often, it must be admitted, the Aegean and the Mediterranean seas. In all the thinking of the Founding Fathers history occupied a central position. History, wrote Benjamin Franklin, would "give occasion to expatiate on the advantage of civil orders and constitutions; how men and their properties are protected by joining in societies and establishing government; their industry encouraged and rewarded; arts invented, and life made more comfortable; the advantages of liberty, mischiefs of licentiousness, benefits arising from good laws, and from a due execution of justice, etc. . . ." Jefferson, too, was confident that history was essential to wisdom and statesmanship. It taught the young, he observed, the virtues of freedom; "by apprizing them of the past it will enable them to judge of the future; it will avail them of the experience of other times and nations, it will qualify them as judges of the actions and designs of men, it will enable them to know ambition under every disguise . . . and, knowing it, to defeat its views." There is no need to multiply examples of anything so familiar.

What is clear, at once, is that the generation of the Enlightenment, European and American alike, thought of history not as we customarily think of it, as the reconstruction of the past, but as a moral enterprise. Perhaps it was not history at all; let us call it philosophy and be done with it. They had no use for the pedantry of the annalists, and the erudites; they ignored Vico and Justus Möser; they would have had little interest in the research of a Niebuhr or a Ranke, both born in the eighteenth century, who addressed themselves to what actually happened.

They were, in short, in the great tradition of historical thinking, and writing—the tradition that stretches almost unbroken from Herodotus to Gibbon—history as philosophy. In the ancient world the philosophy had been predominantly secular; in the Middle Ages it was philosophy as a revelation of God's purpose with man; since the seventeenth century it had once again become covertly, if not always overtly, secular. Bolingbroke had put it with wonderful succinctness: history is philosophy teaching by examples; and what was this but a restatement of the axiom of Dionysius of Halicarnassus? This was Voltaire's notion of history, Voltaire who towered above all of his contemporaries, and Montesquieu's too—the Montesquieu of the *Grandeur and Decadence of Rome;* it was the Abbé Raynal's idea of history, and that of Turgot and his tragic disciple Condorcet; of the Swiss, Johannes Müller, who inspired Schiller's *William Tell* and of the Dane, Ludwig Holberg who wrote *Universal History,* and of the great Gibbon himself, the only one of them who can be called a professional historian.

It was all history as philosophy, not history as fact. "Let us begin by laying facts aside," wrote Rousseau in his *Dissertation on the Inequality of Mankind,* and that is pretty much how all of them began, all but Gibbon and Justus Möser of Osnabrück, anyway. In America too, perhaps especially in America, it was morality that was important, not facts; it was wisdom and justice, and virtue. Here is the eminent Dr. Rush urging the trustees of the new Dickinson College to exchange a set of the *Journals of the House of Commons* for books on mathematics. "It would distress me" he wrote, "to hear that a student at Dickinson College had ever wasted half an hour in examining even their title pages. He would find nothing in them but such things as a scholar and a gentleman should strive to forget." Just before the Revolution John Adams praised Mrs. Macauley's *History of England* because "it is calculated . . . to bestow the reward of virtue, praise, upon the generous and worthy only. . . . No charms of eloquence can atone for the want of this *exact historical morality.*" And just a few months later the young Jefferson was writing that he considered history as a "moral exercise." It was, he added, interchangeable with fiction in inculcating moral lessons.

Now how could the philosophers so confidently rely on history to provide lessons that would be relevant to their own times and their own problems? Easy enough. We have learned to distrust all analogies taken from remote times or different societies, but to the Enlightenment no societies were different and no times remote. After all, mankind was everywhere the same: Hume said it, once and for all: "Mankind are so much the same in all times and places that History informs us of nothing new or strange. . . . Its chief use is only to discover the constant and universal principles of human nature."

Constant and universal: those are the key words. If history was not everywhere the same, human nature was, and it was human nature that the *philosophes* studied. That is why they could move with ease from Greece and Rome to China or Peru. That is why Leibniz could recommend Chinese as the universal language and his disciple Christian Wolff could assert that the teachings of Confucius were quite as acceptable as those of Jesus, a heresy for which he was promptly banished from Prussia by an indignant monarch; that is why Diderot could go to Tahiti for lessons that Bougainville failed to teach, and Dr. Johnson to Abyssinia. That is why the *philosophes* had so little interest in individuals as such, only in individuals as a type, and why the Enlightenment produced so few good biographies: Boswell was, of course, a Romantic, and so too Parson Weems. That is why artists insisted on depersonalizing their historical characters, dressing them all in Roman togas or, perhaps, in nothing—even the practical Franklin wished to be painted "with a gown for his dress and a Roman head." "A history painter paints man in general; a portrait painter a particular man, and consequently a defective model," said Sir Joshua Reynolds, who was magisterial. That is why the eighteenth century—outside England anyway—delighted in the nude, for if you are going to portray Man in General then away with clothing, which was always of time and place. The human body, after all, was the same in every clime and every age.

Thus the Founding Fathers could confidently draw from their study of history, chiefly Greek, Roman, and English, moral lessons that were applicable to their own day. But now we come to something that still has the power to excite us. All read the same history, all drew from its examples much the same body of conclusions. But here the school of Adams and the school of Jefferson parted company. Adams was sure that Americans would repeat all the follies and errors of the past; Jefferson was confident that they might triumph over the past, that in the New World man might begin anew.

It was not Puritanism: Jefferson had no use for the sifted grain thesis, for he thought all human grain potentially good. It was

147

not millennialism—Freneau with his boast that "Paradise anew shall flourish, no second Adam lost"—for Jefferson did not believe in Original Sin and perhaps not in any sin not the product of Law or Religion. There was exultation, to be sure, and hope: "I like the dreams of the future better than the history of the past" he wrote to Adams, who was not much given to dreams. But as with most of Jefferson's ideas, these ideas about history were firmly rooted in logic and experience. For never before had man been vouchsafed a chance to achieve the good life under auspices that were ideal. In America Nature was abundant and, for the most part, benevolent. As Jefferson wrote from Paris to his friend James Monroe:

> I only wish you may find it convenient to come over here.
> . . . It will make you adore your own country, its soil, its climate, its equality, liberty, laws, people and manners. My God! how little do our countrymen know what precious blessings they are in possession of, and which no other people on earth enjoy. I confess I had no idea of it myself. While we shall see multiplied instances of Europeans going to live in America, I will venture to say no man now living will ever see an instance of an American removing to settle in Europe.

And where environment was not beneficent, science could change it, for men were masters of their environment, not its helpless victims—just what Lester Ward was to say almost a century later in his stunning refutation of Herbert Spencer. What is more—another new idea this—Government was part of environment, and men flourished in freedom as they could not under tyranny, flourished in peace as they could not in war, flourished in prosperity as they could not in poverty. So said that stout conservative, the Reverend Ezra Stiles:

Liberty, civil and religious, has sweet and attractive charms. The enjoyment of this, with property, has filled the English settlers in America with a most amazing spirit, which has operated, and still will operate, with great energy. Never before has the experiment been so effectually tried of every man's reaping the fruits of his labor, and feeling his share in the aggregate system of power. The ancient republicks did not stand on the people at large; and therefore no example or precedent can be taken from them. Even men of arbitrary principles will be obliged, if they would figure in these states, to assume the patriot so long that they will at length become charmed with the sweets of liberty.

What is more, learning and science, now to be the possession of all the people, would teach wisdom, solve problems, and confer happiness. This was clear to all thoughtful observers; it was clear, above all, to the scientists. Here is Dr. Ramsey, down in South Carolina, reflecting on the significance of independence:

A large volume of the Book of Nature, yet unread, is open before us. . . . We stand on the shoulders of our predecessors with respect to the arts that depend upon experiment and observation. The face of our country, intersected by rivers, or covered with woods and swamps, gives ample scope for the improvement of mechanicks, mathematics, and natural philosophy.

And he concluded that

the art and sciences, which languished under the low prospects of subjection, will raise their drooping heads. . . . Even now, amidst the tumults of war, literary institutions are forming all over the continent, which must light up such a blaze of knowledge as cannot fail to burn, and catch, and spread, until it has

149

finally illuminated with the rays of science, the most distant retreats of ignorance and barbarity.

In such an environment, and with such prospects, the lessons of the past were irrelevant, or were there only as an example and a warning.

Not content with rejecting the lessons of the past, the Jeffersonians added a new dimension to the idea of Progress, Americanizing that idea, as it were, just as they had Americanized the character of history by making it do service for the future rather than for the past. Progress was a darling notion of the Enlightenment, but progress as the *philosophes* imagined it was a narrow and elitist concept: the advance of arts and letters and the sciences, the conquest of superstition and tyranny. Americans—we cannot assign this to any one group or school, so general it was—democratized and vulgarized the idea. Progress was the welfare of the common man: it was not merely something to delight members of the academies or the courts; it was something to lift the standards of living. It was not merely the avoidance of ancient evils— that could be taken for granted—it was the achievement of positive good. Thus they took progress away from the Utopianists— the fiction writers and the imaginary kingdom-contrivers like Thomas More or Campanella or St. Pierre or Holberg, and placed it squarely in America. They not only democratized it, they realized it; and every *philosophe* in the Old World acknowledged that Utopia was indeed America and differed only on whether it was to be found in Pennsylvania or in Connecticut.

But all this did not mean that Americans were bereft of a past: not at all. Americans had no intention of denying themselves the advantages and pleasures of a past, or of history. Many of the Founding Fathers, Jefferson and Rush, Isaiah Thomas and Jeremy Belknap, were not merely men of the Enlightenment; they were Romantics as well. These two disparate philosophies blended in the Old World as in the New, in a Rousseau and even in Diderot, in Lessing and Kant and, in a fascinating manner, in Goethe. As Romantics they were deeply concerned with the past, for it is the very essence of Romanticism to look to the past, and cherish it.

There was of course a very special reason why Americans needed a past, and that was that they were engaged in creating —bringing forth, as Lincoln put it—a new nation. Nationalism, needless to observe, is political Romanticism, and everywhere, in the Old World as in the New, nationalism immersed itself in a past, real or conjectural, designed to provide an appropriate cultural and psychological foundation. This is not the place to elaborate on the nature of modern nationalism; it is sufficient to say that one of its essential ingredients was a common past. It was an ingredient easy for the French to come by, the Germans, the Italians, the Danes, or, later, the Bohemians, the Irish, the Norwegians. But it was not easy for Americans to come by, for as a people the Americans did not, in fact, have very much of a past. With characteristic energy and resourcefulness they set about repairing this deficiency.

The ingredients were there, to be sure, more ample than one might suppose, more ample, certainly, than those available for the documenting of the origins of most of the Old World nations, for however inadequate the sources for the founding of Virginia or the Bay Colony, they were richer by far than those available for the founding of Rome by Remus and Romulus—or was it Noah?—or of Britain by Gog and Magog, or even by the Angles and Saxons and Jutes.

The materials were there, and the historians, too, let us call them antiquarians and be done with it. Most of them were content with state history, and very good these histories were, too: models, some of them, which we have not yet surpassed; Belknap's *New Hampshire* and Williamson's *North Carolina* and Samuel

Williams's *Vermont* and Ramsay's *South Carolina* among them, and above all Jefferson's *Notes on Virginia*, with its arguments and its eloquence. They were local histories, but with wider implications: with a great deal of what we now call cultural anthropology and with philosophical overtones.

For they were *philosophes*, American type, Belknap and Williamson and Williams and many of the others. They were Romantics, too, those two things blended happily enough in the New World, interested in what was distinctly American because conscious of writing a new page in history. They could, even, be *érudits*, not perhaps as erudite as Muratori down in his archives in Modena, or Peter Suhm in Copenhagen with his library of 125,000 volumes, or that remarkable Johann Jacob Moser of Tübingen who notwithstanding five years in solitary confinement managed to publish 227—or was it 600?—books during a busy life. That was not the American pattern.

As philosophers they drew from history such moral lessons as seemed appropriate to the new nation, and above all the moral lesson that the moral lessons of the past might be irrelevant because Americans were embarked upon something new. As romanticists they were called on to provide an historical past for a people almost without a past, and this task they performed with astonishing success, merging the past with the present so that the Founding Fathers, many of them still alive, came to seem like Jason and the Argonauts, just as even now our cowboys seem like Robin Hood and his men. As scholars they delighted in just such enterprises as those we celebrate still, the collecting of source materials and the founding of historical societies.

When we consider the scanty resources, the want of patronage, official or ecclesiastical, the absense of a learned class, we cannot but be astonished at how well they performed these tasks.

It is all very distant now, and, in an age of technical history, almost alien, this belief that the New World was opening a new chapter in history, that Man was in control of his own destiny, that virtue was the distinguishing character of a republic and that collectively the American people could achieve virtue; this concern for the happiness of man, the progress of society and the prosperity of the Commonwealth. But these were the principles, and the hopes, that animated the generation of Thomas Jefferson; the sentiments, too, that inspired the achievement of independence, the founding of the nation, and the advancement of science and learning, and that provided posterity with the materials by which it could know its forebears.

Yes, it is all very distant now, and we are in a time of disillusionment, one that questions the value of history, the relevance of the past, and the achievement of the Founding Fathers. Our history now is increasingly history as recrimination and history as indictment. Perhaps something is to be said for the simple and naive views of the past. Let us conclude with a passage from one of the letters of Thomas Paine, who so wonderfully combined the spirit of rationalism—did he not write *Common Sense* and *The Age of Reason?*—with romanticism—was he not prosecuted for his defense of the *Rights of Man?* He had no sense of history—Edmund Burke made that clear in his *Reflections*—but he had a feeling for the future denied the great Burke.

A thousand years hence, perhaps in less, America may be what Europe is now. The innocence of her character that won the hearts of all nations in her favor may sound like a romance, and her inimitable virtue as if it had never been. . . . The ruin of that liberty which thousands bled for or struggled to obtain may just furnish materials for a village tale.

When we contemplate the fall of empires and the extinction of the nations of the ancient world, we see but little to excite our regret but the mouldering ruins of pompous palaces, magnificent museums, lofty pyramids, and walls and towers of the most costly workmanship. But when the empire of America shall fall, the subject for contemplative sorrow will be infinitely greater than crumbling brass and marble can inspire. It will not then be said, here stood a temple of vast antiquity, here rose a Babel of invisible height, or there a palace of sumptuous extravagance, but here, ah painful thought, the noblest work of human wisdom, the grand scheme of human glory, the fair cause of freedom, rose and fell.

7

THE ORIGINS
AND NATURE OF
AMERICAN
NATIONALISM

THERE had been nations long before the American and the French Revolutions, but the rise of self-conscious nationalism, cultural, linguistic, and psychological, as well as political, is largely a product of the past two centuries. Into the insoluble questions of the ultimate origins of nationalism we need not enter. There are historians who discern elements of nationalism in the Greek City States, others who date nationalism from the barbarian invasions, still others who prefer the ninth century, the Crusades, or the Hundred Years War. But even those insistent on the earlier origins of nationalism will concede that the nationalism of the late eighteenth and the early nineteenth centuries represented something new in history, and that much of what we now think of as nationalism is a product of this modern period. Beginning with the French Revolution older nations—France herself, for example, the Denmark of Grundtvig, the Germany of Fichte, the Norway of Wergeland, the Switzerland of Johann Bodmer—experienced a new birth of nationalism. And all through the nineteenth century nations struggled toward birth as states, and states disintegrated into nations, as people conscious of a common language, culture, and history strove to transform cultural and historical nationalism into political nationalism, or to give older and artificial political organizations new and more meaningful form. Thus with Greece and Serbia in the early years of the century; the states of Latin America in the second and third decades; Belgium in the 1830s; and Germany, Italy, Rumania, Bohemia, Norway, and Finland in subsequent years. Thus, in the twentieth century, with India and Pakistan, the Arab states, and many of the new nations of Asia and Africa. One culmination of all this—in the opinion of some historians a regrettable one—was the Wilsonian doctrine of self-determination written into the peace settlements after the First World War; another—and more sobering—climacteric is the wave of nationalism that has brought some sixty new nations into existence since 1945.

Against this background of renascent or emerging nationalism, the American experience after 1775 appears familiar and unexceptional, a natural part of an harmonious pattern. In one sense this is proper enough: after all, many of the same impulses of nationalism and romanticism, democracy and reform that quickened the mind and spirit of peoples of Old World nations affected the American people. And the same powerful forces of economy—the industrial revolution, railroads, the corporate device, electricity and the dynamo—that operated on peoples and nations in nineteenth-century Europe operated in America, sometimes with double force.

Yet the American experience differed profoundly from that of the nations of the Old World. Far from being merely an extension of past history, or a realization of accumulated potentialities, cultural, social, and religious, America reversed the familiar processes of history and inaugurated a new philosophy and a new mechanism of nation-making.

This was the view of one of the most sagacious of American

statesmen, John Adams, and we may take as our point of departure what he wrote to his friend Hezekiah Niles in 1818:

> The colonies had grown up under constitutions of government so different, there was so great a variety of religions, they were composed of so many different nations, their customs, manners and habits had so little resemblance, and their intercourse had been so rare, and their knowledge of each other so imperfect, that to unite them in the same principles in theory and the same system of action, was certainly a very difficult enterprise. The complete accomplishment of it in so short a time, and by such simple means, was perhaps a singular example in the history of mankind. *Thirteen clocks were made to strike together—a perfection of mechanism which no artist had ever before effected.*

Because thirteen American states hugging the Atlantic seaboard became a single nation, spanning a continent and embracing forty-nine continental states, we take American nationalism for granted. But there was nothing foreordained about this triumph of nationalism and consolidation. Why did not the vast territory between Canada and the Caribbean go the way of South America, or Africa in modern times? After all Spanish America, with a common origin, language, culture, and religion, frag-

*Could John Adams have seen the letter from Jeremy Belknap to Ebenezer Hazard of 3 March 1784? "Comparisons sometimes illustrate subjects; but where can one be found to illuminate this? Imagine, my friend, thirteen independent clocks, going all together by the force of their own weights, and carrying thirteen *independent* hammers fitted to strike *one bell.* If you can so nicely wind and adjust all these clocks as to make them move exactly alike, and strike at the same instant, you will have indeed a most curious and regular beating of time; but if there be ever so small a deviation from the point of identity, who will be able to know the hour by the sound of such an automaton?

"The plain English of all this is that our present form of federal government appears to be inadequate to the purpose for which it was instituted" (Collections Mass. Hist. Soc.).

mented into twenty states, while Africa achieved a kind of travesty of modern nationalism by giving birth to a litter of seventeen nations in a single year.

Though important ingredients of nationalism were present in the American colonies in the 1770s, they had yet to be animated and organized; others, no less important, were lacking. To many contemporaries the forces that threatened the security of the new nation appeared more formidable than those that promised it prosperity. Thus the Loyalist Jonathan Boucher—not an unbiased observer, to be sure—reminded his quondam countrymen, correctly enough, that "a great and durable republic is certainly a new thing in the world," and prophesied its speedy dissolution. The unfriendly Earl of Sheffield observed in 1783 of the then American West that "the authority of Congress can never be maintained over those distant and boundless regions, and her nominal subjects will speedily imitate and multiply examples of independence," and he formulated economic policies designed to vindicate his dour predictions. Turgot, too—not only an economist, but a philosopher of Progress and a friend to America—thought the forces of disintegration stronger than those of integration. "In the general union of the provinces among themselves," he wrote his friend Dr. Price, "I do not see a coalition, a fusion of all the parts, making but one body, one and homogeneous. It is only an aggregation of parts, always too much separated and preserving always a tendency to division by the diversity of their laws, their manners, their opinions . . . still more by the inequality of their actual forces. It is only a copy of the Dutch Republic, but this Republic had not to fear, as the American Republic has, the possible enlargement of some of its provinces." The malevolent Montmorin said the same thing in one of his dispatches to Louis Otto: "It appears that in all the American provinces there is more or less tendency towards a

democracy; ... The result will be that the confederation will have
little stability, and that by degrees the different states will subsist
in perfect independence of each other." This was written in
August 1787! The English clerical economist, Dean Josiah
Tucker, was no less impatient with the claims of American na-
tionalists:

> As to the future grandeur of America and its being a rising
> empire under one head . . . it is one of the idlest and most
> visionary notions that ever was conceived, even by writers of
> romance. When those immense inland regions beyond the
> back settlements are taken into account, they form the highest
> probability that the Americans never can be united into one
> empire, under any species of government whatever. Their fate
> seems to be a disunited people till the end of time (*Cui Bono*).

Thirty years later Sydney Smith, of the rancorous *Edinburgh
Review*, was still asserting that America could not possibly remain one nation:

> The Americans are a very sensible reflecting people and have
> conducted their affairs extremely well, but it is scarcely possi-
> ble to conceive that such an empire should very long remain
> undivided, or that the dwellers on the Columbia should have
> common interest with the navigators of the Hudson and the
> Delaware.

And Tocqueville's prediction—a prediction made in the face of
his own reasoning and his own evidence—is familiar enough:

> Whatever faith I may have in the perfectability of man, until
> human nature is altered, and man wholly transformed, I shall
> refuse to believe in the duration of a government which is
> called upon to hold together forty different peoples, dis-
> seminated over a territory equal to one half of Europe in ex-

tent, to avoid all rivalry, ambition and struggles between them, and to direct their independent activity to the accomplishment of the same designs.

Nor were these bleak predictions merely an expression of foreign hostility to the American experiment. Some Americans— not many to be sure—were as skeptical as were the Old World critics. Speaking in the Constitutional Convention Nathaniel Gorham of Massachusetts observed that there was no danger that popular representation would ever produce too large a legislative body, for "it is not to be supposed that the Government will last so long as to produce this effect. Can it be supposed that this vast Country including the Western territory will 150 years hence remain one nation?" And the somewhat perverse Gouverneur Morris who had been a member of the Convention remembered later that "fond as the framers of our national Constitution were of Republican government, they were not so much blinded by their attachment as not to discern the difficulty, perhaps impracticability, of raising a durable ediface from crumbling materials. History, the parent of political science, had told them that it was almost as vain to expect permanency from democracy, as to construct a palace on the surface of the sea."

In the minds of all observers—the hopeful and the cynical alike —was the tenacity and persistence of local attachments, those local and regional attachments which did, in the end, disrupt the Union. Which would prove stronger: loyalty to the state or to the new nation? Virginians—Jefferson himself—long spoke of the old dominion as their "nation." What John Adams later recalled —how difficult it was for thirteen clocks to strike together—was clear enough to many contemporaries. Thomas Pownall, who had been governor of three American colonies (New York, Massachusetts, and South Carolina), predicted that "the different manner in which they [the colonies] are settled, the different modes of government they possess, the various principles of repulsion they create, the different interests . . . the religious interests . . . the rivalship and jealousies which arise from hence, and the impracticability if not the impossibility of reconciling and accommodating these impossible ideas and claims, will keep them forever separate." Lewis Morris provided in his will that his son Gouverneur should never set foot in the neighbouring colony of Connecticut "lest he imbibe that low cunning so incident to the people of that country," and half a century later James Fenimore Cooper, in his novel *Satanstoe*, put into the mouth of the aristocratic Mrs. Littlepage the observation that "I should have sent Evans to Yale had it not been for the miserable manner of speaking English they have in New England, and I have no wish to have a son of mine who might pass for a Cornishman."

We must not, however, exaggerate the importance of these expressions of mutual distrust. More important, as it turned out, were the habits of intercolonial cooperation—institutions like the American Philosophical Society; enterprises like intercolonial wars and the struggle against the Indian; religious denominations and loyalties, especially among the dissenting churches; the habit of study at out-of-colony colleges; a flourishing postal service; newspapers that circulated from colony to colony, and books as well—*Poor Richard's Almanac*, for example—all of those things which made it not only possible but plausible for Patrick Henry to exclaim in 1775 that "the distinctions between Virginians, Pennsylvanians, New Yorkers and New Englanders are no more," and for Thomas Paine to write that "our citizenship in the United States is our national character. . . . Our great title is AMERICANS." But who could be sure of this, at the time?

It might, then, have gone either way, this bold experiment in nation-making. We take for granted that the outcome of all this turmoil and struggle was a single, united, nation, but should not.

Rather we should ask, how did it happen that a people which confessed such heterogeneous racial stocks, such varied soils and climates, such diverse and often competing economic interests, such miscellaneous religious patterns, achieved a stable and enduring national character with an ease that confounded not only the expectations of critics, but of history as well? In the Old World, with its century-long traditions of feudalism and dynastic nationalism and its interdependence of Church and State, the particular triumphed over the general. In the New World—the North American part of it, Canada as well as the United States —the general triumphed over the particular. In the Old World, territory was fragmented, and economies, cultures, languages, and religions followed divergent and conflicting paths. In North America the fragmentation under way everywhere in the seventeenth and eighteenth centuries was arrested, and—in North America—succeeded by concentration and unity.

One important consideration in all this is that the United States developed almost wholly in the era of, and under the auspices of, the industrial revolution, and that the unification of the vast American territory was a product of that revolution. But Latin America, too, came to maturity during the era of the industrial revolution without consequent unification, and even twentieth-century economy and technology have not been powerful enough to induce the tiny states of Central America to unite. In Europe, too, the industrial revolution has not mitigated national fragmentation. Scotland adhered to England before the rise of modern industry and transportation, but the most persuasive economic considerations have not yet induced Northern and Southern Ireland to drop their differences. Norway was once part of the Kingdom of Denmark and so, too, Skåne, while Finland was long part of Sweden, but Scandinavia was probably as close to unification in the reign of Frederick II of Denmark as it is today. The industrial revolution has not induced

Belgium to rejoin France nor Portugal Spain. Nor is there any persuasive evidence that industrialism is making for the unification of Asia; so far, except in China, the tendency is in the other direction. Consider, too, that the foundations of American nationalism were firmly laid before the full impact of the industrial revolution, and that it is possible to argue that the industrial revolution contributed rather to the break-up than to the cohesion of the union in 1860.

What then is the explanation of the fulfillment of American nationalism, a phenomenon so astonishing that to many Americans of the time—and since—it seemed Providential: as Dr. Ramsay asserted—he was an historian as well as a scientist, and so deserves our confidence—"the special interposition of Providence in our behalf makes it impious to disbelieve in the final establishment of our Heaven-protected independence" (Oration on the Advantages of American Independence). Washington made it all but official in his Farewell Address. "No people," he said, "can be bound to acknowledge and adore the invisible Hand which conducts the affairs of man more than those of the United States. Every step by which we have advanced to the character of an independent nation seems to have been distinguished by some token of Providential agency." The evidence is indeed so overwhelming that it must be regarded as conclusive. Let us restrict ourselves to one more authoritative statement, that by the Reverend Timothy Dwight, President of Yale College and widely regarded as the Pope of New England: "In all the changes which have befallen our native country, the interpositions of Divine Providence in its behalf have been wonderful. . . . Who gave the artillery of your enemies into the hands of Manly; and their ammunition into those of Mugford? Who surrendered to you the armies of Burgoyne? . . . Who established on solid grounds your independence and your peace? And set your feet in a broad place, a possession rich, secure and immense? Who has filled your veins with health and your garners with all manner of store?"

The most famous explanation is also the most nearly accurate. "Our fathers," said President Lincoln, "brought forth a new nation." American nationalism was a creative act, the product of the deliberate application of will and intelligence by statesmen, soldiers, scholars, men of letters, jurists, artists, scientists, explorers, and of the farmers and seamen and workingmen who made up the body of the people. Where, in most Old World countries, the social, cultural, religious, and psychological foundations of nationalism were laid long before the political superstructure was built, in the United States the political structure came first and the rest had to be added. The United States started as a national state and was confronted at once with the task of vindicating the political decision—first on the field of battle, then in the arena of economy, society, language, culture, and sentiment.

When the long traditions of English, French, Danish or Swedish nationalism—traditions of language, law, religion and history —are compared with what America had in 1775 or in 1789, the contrast is clear and even dramatic. In those countries where political nationalism was very old—like England or France—the nation grew out of well-cultivated soil and long processes of cultural integration; in short, out of history. And similarly most of the "new" nations of the nineteenth and early twentieth century—Belgium, Serbia, Italy, Germany, Norway, Poland, Czechoslovakia, India, Ireland, and Israel—had long traditions of cultural nationalism and sometimes of political, stretching back into the distant past, before they crystallized into modern states.

Instinctively, and consciously too, the American of the Revolutionary generation set about to create a new nation and to furnish it with a common body of laws, literature, education, history, heroes, symbols, myths, and traditions—with all those ingredients customarily associated with nationalism. As Thomas Paine said—Paine who himself contributed so much to the making of the new nation—"a new era for politics is struck, a new method of thinking hath arisen."

It was indeed a new era, and it did require a new method of thinking. So said young Noah Webster, of dictionary fame, who pointed out that "America is an independent empire and *ought* to assume a national character. Nothing," he added, "can be more ridiculous than servile imitation of the manners, the language, and the vices of foreigners. For America in her infancy to adopt the present maxims of the Old World, would be to stamp the wrinkles of decrepit age upon the bloom of youth and to plant the seeds of decay in a vigorous constitution." And in 1788 he exhorted his fellow-countrymen to "unshackle your minds, and act like independent beings. . . . You have an empire to raise and support by your exertions, and a national character to establish and extend by your wisdom and virtue." And Alexander Hamilton, not always enthusiastic for home-grown products, assured his friend Rufus King that "we are laboring hard to establish in this country principles more and more national, and free from all foreign ingredients, so that we may be neither Greeks nor Trojans but truly Americans." Jefferson's friend, Dr. Rush, wished American youth to be taught that "the chains which have bound the science of government in Europe are unloosed in America. Here it is open to investigation and improvement."

In America, at least, nationalism implied improvement, even required it. Colonel John Parke, who had turned from soldiering to poetry, improved on Horace by substituting American for Roman scenes and Washington for Augustus. Improvement was in the mind of Nicholas Pike, too, who pointed out in the preface to his *Arithmetic* of 1788 that "as the United States are now an independent nation, it was judged that a system might be calculated more suitable to our Meridian than those heretofore published." His rival, Erastus Root, who boldly adopted the new decimal system, was even more outspoken:

> Let us . . . no longer meanly follow the British intricate way of reckoning. Let them have their own way, and us ours. Their mode is suited to the genius of their government—for it seems to be the policy of tyrants to keep their accounts in as intricate and perplexing a method as possible. . . . But Republican money ought to be simple, and adapted to the meanest capacity. . . .

Gastronomy, too, was to yield to the logic of nationalism. Over in the Savoy Joel Barlow sang the praises of Hasty Pudding, carefully explaining that "a simplicity of diet, whether it be considered with reference to the happiness of the individual or the prosperity of a nation, is of more consequence than we are apt to imagine." And a few years later (1796) one Amelia Simmons brought out an *American Cookery*, "adapted," as she said, "to all Grades of life," and proudly including recipes for Indian Pudding, Johnny Cake, Slapjacks, and Pompkin (sic) Pie.

Even geography was to be given a nationalist slant, and the Reverend Robert Davidson, who was not only a clergyman but an historian and poet as well, and who later improved the Bible by recasting it into verse, was inspired to flaunt his national pride in doggerel:

> We'll now take our stand,
> On this happy, prolific, and widespreading land,
> Where Nature has wrought with a far nobler hand.
> No more let the Old World be proud of her mountains,
> Her rivers, her mines, her lakes, and her fountains,
> Tho' great in themselves, they no longer appear
> To be great, when compared, with the great that are here.
> > *Geography Epitomized:*
> > or *A Tour Round the World*, 1784

This theme, that American Nature was superior to Nature in the Old World, was one of which Americans never tired. Thus in 1785 a contributor to the Columbian Magazine hoped that "we shall have poets that will *eternize* in song, their native groves and rivers." Why, he asked, "may we not yet see our rivers as superior to the babbling brooks of the old continent in fame as in size, when neither the Roman Tiber nor the British Thames shall surpass the gentle Schulkill [sic] or the majestic Delaware." And that same year John Adams, then unhappily in London, confided similar sentiments to his Diary. "It will be long, I hope, before Ridings, Parks, Pleasure grounds, Gardens and ornamented Farms grow so much in fashion in America; but Nature has done greater Things and furnished nobler Materials there: the Oceans, Islands, Rivers, Mountains, Valleys, are all laid out upon a larger Scale."

Nature was not only grander and more sublime in America, but more benevolent as well—quite a reversal, this, from the arguments of the Comte de Buffon and the Abbé Raynal and that other Abbé, the wretched Corneille de Pauw—who had condemned the whole of the New World to degeneracy. Here is the sensible Abigail Adams, writing to her sister Elizabeth Shaw:

> Do you know that European birds have not half the melody of ours? Nor is their fruit half so sweet, nor their flowers half so fragrant, nor their manners half so pure, nor their people half so virtuous. . . .

"Keep this to yourself," Abigail added, but how could any American keep this to himself? Already the word went out, it was the new gospel: Everything is better in America: God more benevolent, Nature more prodigal, Man more virtuous.

Not only was Nature better in the New World; Man, too, was better. It is one of the most familiar themes of Jeffersonian philosophy, and it persisted long after Jefferson in literature, philosophy, and politics. The "American Farmer," Hector St. Jean de Crèvecoeur, made it clear in his famous *Letters:* "Men are like plants; the goodness and flavor of the fruit proceeds from the peculiar soil in which they grow." The American is a new man, who has foresworn the past: he "acts upon new principles; he must therefore entertain new ideas and form new opinions." That is what Tom Paine said in his reply to the strictures of the Abbé Raynal: "Our style and manner of thinking have undergone a revolution more extraordinary than the political revolution of the country. We see with other eyes; we hear with other ears; we think with other thoughts than those we formerly used." The "American Homer," Joel Barlow, summed it up in felicitous lines:

> Here social man a second birth shall find,
> And a new range of reason lift his mind,
> Feed his strong intellect with purer light,
> A nobler sense of duty—and of right.

And remember Jefferson's exultant letter to Joseph Priestley just after his inauguration to the Presidency:

> We can no longer say there is nothing new under the sun. For this whole chapter in the history of man is new. The great extent of our republic is new. Its sparse habitation is new. The mighty wave of public opinion which has rolled over it is new. . . .

Clearly, then, Americans had the instinct for nationality. How did they transform the instinct into reality?

*

National unity for the vast area now embraced in the continental United States was not foreordained. Americans lacked, in the beginning, some of the important ingredients which had long

been thought essential to nationalism. Just what are those ingredients is still a matter of dispute, but there is general agreement on the most essential. Almost every list includes a political
framework, a people who desire to belong to one nation, a common language, a territory, a body of traditions, and a history. To
these an earlier generation would add a common religion, and
ours a viable economy. None of these requirements is absolute.
Switzerland survives with three languages, Belgium and Canada
with two; and until recently the Jews had no territory at all; India
lacks a common religion and modern communist states have substituted an ideology for religion; and a sobering number of the
new African states do not seem to have a viable economy. The
United States began life with three or four of the ingredients
thought most essential, but they had them on trust, as it were;
they were still to be vindicated. The others, equally important,
had to be acquired.

The United States did have a people who—except the Loyalists
—wanted to be Americans; it possessed a common language; it
inherited common traditions of law and politics; it had common
social institutions and practices. But an effective political organization had yet to be built; the territorial basis was uncertain, and
had to be fixed; the history and traditions had yet to be formed;
and both the religious and the economic interests were so diverse
that they might become competitive and even antagonistic. Some
of the other ingredients customarily associated with nationalism
in the Old World were wholly lacking: a monarch, a ruling class,
an established church, an army and navy and national antipathies, a national capital, and, as Henry James later observed, even
a distinctive national name.

Let us look at this process of nation-making through the eyes
of 1776 or 1787, when almost everything remained to be done,
rather than of a later day, when almost everything had been done.
Consider, first, the major ingredients which the new nation did

possess: people, language, territory, political traditions, keeping always in mind that these were conditional, that—to use John Adams's phrase—they existed *in posse* rather than *in esse.*

"People," we take for granted, yet in the light of the prodigious movements of population in the Second World War and post-war years, we should not. What crimes the Germans perpetrated to obtain a united people, what wholesale transplantings and genocide! What fantastic shiftings-about of populations since 1945—twelve million Germans from the East to the West, Poles and Russians, Czechs, Austrians, Germans, Italians, Hindus and Moslems, Chinese and Vietnamese, Arabs and Jews, shuttled around by the million. Nor is this a phenomenon of the mid-twentieth century only, though it was in the past generation that it took on gigantic proportions. Think of the efforts of the Germans, the French, the Russians, the Italians, the Turks in the nineteenth century to get a homogeneous population, or to extend their dominion over all peoples of their own ethnic group, to force all who were not nationals into a nationalistic pattern.

Now after the initial tragedy of the expulsion, or flight, of the Loyalists, the United States had no population problem of this kind. The American people of the 1780s were in fact heterogeneous, but as Crèvecoeur observed in one of the most familiar of his Letters, the New World made its inhabitants *Americans* overnight: *"ubi panis ibi patria."* This was in part good fortune—the good fortune of isolation and open land—but it was in part policy, too: the policy of easy naturalization, social and cultural assimilation, religious and class toleration, and general education. The habit of speedy transformation of Irish and German, Norwegian and Jew into American persisted and flourished, triumphing over all of the countermovements of Naturalization Acts, Know-Nothingism, and Nativism. Notwithstanding an immigration that numbered eventually over forty millions (and except for the Negroes who constitute a shocking exception) the

United States has never confessed any unassimilable blocs of foreigners who have rejected America or been rejected by America. All through the nineteenth century the laws, at least, vindicated the sentiment expressed by Emma Lazarus in the poem inscribed on the Statue of Liberty. More important—in the light of the requirements for nationalism—the immigrants who flooded into the United States were almost pathetically eager to shuffle off their old allegiances, habits, and languages and be part of the American national experiment. In the perspective of history a common American people is almost as much a creation as is a common history and tradition.

Second, there was—and is—a common language. It is the language of the mother country (for the notion that American English differs in any important way from English English is an invention of British travelers who could tolerate dialects in Yorkshire or Devon but not in America). There were protests against the inheritance, to be sure, but these were eccentric or fanciful. Yet even at the time of independence the common American language was, in some part at least, an achievement and not just a fact of history. Substantial numbers of Americans were of non-English stock, even in the eighteenth century, and their numbers grew; but schools, newspapers, and the pressures of an equalitarian society brought about a general familiarity with English even among those with non-English backgrounds. It was fortunate that the new nation was able to start off with a common language, and with one so rich and flexible, for in time the majority of the American people were to be of non-British stock. But this majority, drawn from every nation of the Old World, and some of the New, has made, for all practical purposes, no contribution to the American language.

But how achieve uniformity over so vast an area? There was, after all, no uniformity in the speech of the European peoples; not only did each region of England, France, the Germanies,

Italy, Spain, even Denmark, have its own distinct dialect, but each class had its own speech and in some countries still does. But national unity required a speech that transcended region and proclaimed freedom from class. So thought John Adams, and bemused by the distinction of the French Academy, he proposed that Congress found a National Institute to "refine and improve" the language in America. This proved not only impracticable, but unnecessary. The public school—taught as often as not by some wandering schoolmaster from some distant region; Webster's Blue-backed Spellers, his Readers, his *American Dictionary;* and eventually Nature herself, by encouraging mobility—imposed the same speech on native and foreign-born alike.* The children, in turn, taught the parents, for America reversed not only the hierarchy of class, but of family. In America the children, not the parents, have always had the whip hand, and for the valid reason that in America, and perhaps only here, it could be taken for granted that each new generation was better educated and more sophisticated than its parents. And in America too— how glaring the contrast with the Old World—there was no permanent difference between the literary language and the vernacular. There were no regional dialects—or none that counted —and no class dialects. We take this for granted now, but how astonishing it was in the world of the eighteenth century. Then a Londoner would with difficulty understand a Yorkshireman and would fail to understand a Scotsman; a Danish gentleman did not speak Danish, but German and French; a German baron could not converse with a peasant, and few Tuscans cared to make the effort to understand a Neopolitan or a Sicilian. But from Maine to Georgia Americans of all classes and ranks (terms

*The German scientist Johann Schoepf noted this as early as the 1780s: "Grown people come over from Germany," he said, "forget their mother tongue . . . while seeking in vain to learn the new speech, and those born in the country hardly ever learn their own language" (*Travels in the Confederation*).

they would scarcely have understood) spoke the same language, and Berkshire lawyers like Joseph Hawley or frontier politicians like Patrick Henry could teach a thing or two about eloquence to a Governor Bowdoin or a Governor Randolph.

The third, and perhaps the most elementary basis for nationalism, is territory. We take American territorial unity for granted now, but logically there was no more reason the territory now embraced in the United States should be a single country than that the territory of South America should be organized into a single country. There was an American land, to be sure, but in 1783 it was immense, and much of it was still to be explored, discovered, surveyed, organized, settled—and vindicated.

What, after all, was the territorial basis of the nation? Was it the territory actually settled, as in most Old World countries? If so it was a comparatively small area, for even the Atlantic seaboard was far from settled by the close of the Revolutionary War, and only tiny pockets of settlements could be found on the western side of the Appalachians. Was it the extensive territory acquired by the Treaty of Paris, westward to the Mississippi—some of it still in dispute between the United States, Britain and Spain, and still occupied, for the most part, by Indians who were uncooperative? Was it the continental domain acquired with such unprecedented speed by treaty with France, by force from Spain, by agreement with Britain, by war with Mexico?

Was not a territory so immense an invitation to dispersion and fragmentation rather than an encouragement to unity? All the Founding Fathers had read Montesquieu, and all knew his reading of history: that while a despot might rule over a large territory a republic must, by definition, be small. Certainly this was the first instance in history of the attempt to create a republic which was large, and it is not surprising that the attempt inspired widespread misgivings. The United States was born the largest nation in the western world; no wonder John Winthrop of Mas-

sachusetts could write that "the idea of an uncompounded republic, on an average one thousand miles in length and eight hundred in breadth, is contrary to the whole experience of mankind." So, too, thought Patrick Henry, who asserted that
republican government on a continental scale was "a work too
great for human wisdom." So said Henry's ally, John Dawson,
who had taken Montesquieu to heart, and who asked rhetorically
"whether any country as extensive as North America . . . can be
governed under one consolidated plan except by the introduction
of despotic principles." Benjamin Rush, always of a suspicious
mind, went so far as to suggest that British territorial cessions to
the new nation were really part of a diabolical plot. "There is but
one path that can lead the United States to destruction," he wrote
in 1787, "and that is their extent of territory. It was probably to
effect this that the British ceded us so much waste land."* Jefferson, animated by the loftiest of motives, confessed to Dr. Priestley that "whether we remain in one confederacy or form into
Atlantic and Mississippi confederations, I believe not very important to the happiness of either part." Almost half a century
later Gallatin, who knew the West as well as any statesman of his
time, could confess that "I have often thought that we boasted too
much of the immense extent of our territory which . . . carries
within itself the seeds of dissolution, by expanding weakens the
bonds of union and the devotedness of true patriotism, and in the
meanwhile destroys the charm of local attachment, separates
friends, and disperses to the most distant quarters members of
the same family."

The convulsive challenge of the 1860s suggests that this might
indeed have happened. Yet we can see now that the fears of a

*There was a grain of truth here. Shelburne's readiness to cede the Northwest
Territory to the United States was inspired not by affection for the new nation
but by the conviction that a United States preoccupied with the settlement of the
West would never be a serious commercial or industrial competitor to Britain.
(See Harlow, I, *Founding of the Second British Empire*, Chaps. v–viii.)

Winthrop, a Henry, a Rush, and others were not justified. Territorial growth more rapid and more extensive than that of any modern nation (except perhaps seventeenth-century Russia) did not make for disunity, but strengthened unity. Instead of fragmenting the nation, it diffused nationalism, and instead of accentuating particularism it encouraged the generalization of nationalism.

How was this achieved? We associate the geographical unity of the new United States with highways and steamboats and railroads, with the mingling of peoples on successive frontiers, and with the development of complementary economies in different regions of the nation. All of these contributed, but none of the contributions would have been possible without the enlightened colonial policies which Americans adopted at the very threshold of nation-making. Old World nations were irremediably committed to the notion that colonies existed for the benefit of their mother countries, and none had been able to solve its colonial problem. "The provinces of absolute monarchies," wrote the great David Hume, "are always better treated than those of free states," but the United States proved that the opposite was true. The United States was, in fact, the greatest colonizing nation of the nineteenth century, and with the most extensive colonies— eventually the whole continent from the Alleghenies to the Pacific. She solved the intractable colonial problem by the simplest of all methods—that is by eliminating colonies, and all in one decade, by a few routine resolutions and laws: the Congressional Resolution of 1780, the Land Ordinances of 1784 and 1785, the Northwest Ordinance of 1787, and the liberal provisions of the Constitution for the admission of new states. How simple it all was, once you accepted the notion that colonies are not inferior, but "distinct republican States" with "the same rights of sovereignty, freedom and independence as the other States," and their inhabitants not colonials, but free and equal citizens.

177

One consequence of the rapid growth of territory and population has been that American love of country has, outside New
England and the South, been a generalized affair. How illuminating that observation of John Quincy Adams, whose roots went
deep into the soil of Massachusetts, apropos the secession of
Maine: "If I were a man of Massachusetts I should deeply lament
this dismemberment of my native state. But the longer I live the
stronger I find my national feelings grow upon me, and the less
my affections are compassed by partial localities." Virginians
could speak of their Commonwealth as "our country," and a later
generation of southerners could take their stand in Dixie Land
to live and die in Dixie. Yet even southerners have been known
to migrate to the North or the West, and elsewhere few Americans have had that passionate attachment to a particular soil or
region so common in England, France, Norway, or Switzerland.
Americans have a rich regional literature, but much of it is a
tribute to the passing of genuine regionalism rather than an
expression of it, and they have nothing to compare to the English
literature of countryside and village, the loving study of field and
road and brook, the curious histories of cricket in Steeple Bump-
stead or fly-casting on the Dart, the voluminous studies of local
dialect and place-names. Alexander Wilson, who knew Britain
almost as well as he knew America, noted this in one of his early
poems:

> Bare bleak heaths and brooks of half a mile,
> Can rouse the thousand bards of Britain's isle.
> There scarce a stream creeps down its narrow bed,
> There scarce a hillock lifts its little head
> Or humble hamlet peeps their glades among
> But lives and murmurs in immortal song.
> "The Foresters"

Boys and girls in the prairie states of America, as in the arid Southwest, sing with rapture "we love thy rocks and rills, thy woods and templed hills," though they cannot conjure up a rill or a templed hill, even in imagination; they take for granted that New England belongs to them as truly as the prairies or the mountains. This worked both ways, and Franklin Roosevelt of Hyde Park acknowledged that his favorite song was *Home on the Range.*

"We have so much country," wrote Nathaniel Hawthorne to his friend Longfellow in 1837, "that we really have no country at all" and he sounded the same note again as late as 1862: "In the vast extent of our country, too vast by far to be taken into one small human heart, we inevitably limit to our own State, or at farthest to our own little section, that sentiment of physical love for the soil which renders an Englishman so intensely sensitive to the dignity and well-being of his little island."

Some foreign observers came to the same conclusion. The Scotsman Charles Mackay observed in 1837 of the American that "his affections have more to do with the social and political system than with the soil he inhabits. The man whose attachments converge upon a particular spot of earth is miserable if removed from it, but give the American his institutions and he cares little where you place him."

Much of this was a product of pioneering experience, of the habit of using up land, and moving on, of delight in the open road, and wandering with the wind. Much of it, too, was a product of large-scale immigration; the break, once and for all, with the ancient soil, the uprooting which was never altogether a transplanting. The pioneer learned to cherish whatever land he cultivated, while he cultivated it, but he could not afford to develop a lasting sentiment about it.

> Woodman, spare that tree!
> Touch not a single bough!
> In youth it sheltered me,
> And I'll protect it now.

wrote the forgotten Knickerbocker poet, George Morris, but the American woodman cut or burned off the forest with a ruthlessness without parallel in history. The pioneer learned to think of whatever place he occupied as a new Eden or Babylon, until he found a better one, which he invariably did next year or the year after. Nor did the immigrants of a later day tend to form deep local attachments; yet if they could not passionately love the slums of New York, the coal mines of Scranton, or the stockyards of Chicago, they might quite sincerely love the whole country.

Americans were fortunate in having a fourth common denominator that contributed to the nurture of nationalism: law and the machinery of government. The common law obtained in all the American colonies: everywhere Americans made contracts, wrote wills, interpreted marriage obligations, and punished crimes in substantially the same way. Without debate they provided, in the Articles of Confederation, for interstate comity: "full faith and credit" in all records and judicial proceedings, and "the privileges and immunities" of citizens, from state to state—precepts carried over into the Constitution. Americans not only took over the common law, but they took it over despite themselves, for after independence there was a sharp reaction against law that had developed in Britain, against Blackstone and Mansfield and the whole body of English admiralty law. Americans yearned for an "American" law, or for Roman law, or for codification, but all in vain.* The common law was so deeply implanted that it triumphed over all rivals, and soon it was strength-

---

*There were, to be sure, modifications in such matters as inheritance, labor and apprenticeship laws, penal law, the rights and privileges of churches, and admiralty.

ened by an imported Equity which, under the noble patronage of Justice Story, became juridically if not legally all but universal.

On the whole, too, the colonies shared a common body of political principles and experience. Americans had never known tyranny, as the Irish had known it, for example, or the Germans; they had larger experience in self-government than any other people. All rejoiced in representative assemblies, the jury system, and a considerable latitude of freedom of speech and of religion. What Roger Williams had said in 1654 was still true more than a century later: "We have long been free from the yoke of wolfish bishops. . . . We have not felt the new chains of Presbyterian tyrants. . . . We have not known what an excise means. We have almost forgotten what titles are. . . . We have long drunk of the cup of as great liberties as any people under the whole heaven." So when Americans came together from different states to make a confederation or Constitution, and to make a nation, they spoke the same language and used the same grammar of politics. Nothing more impressive than this in the continental congresses that met after 1774, or in the Constitutional Convention of 1787. No preliminaries were necessary to enable Committees of Correspondence to function the same way in Massachusetts and in Virginia, or to permit Jefferson and Franklin and John Adams to collaborate on the Declaration of Independence, or to permit Pinckney and Wilson and Sherman to work for common ends in the great Convention. And how interesting that we debated for a century the authorship of the Federalist Papers; we have a uniform society today, but if Eisenhower, Stevenson, and Nixon had collaborated on a comparable body of Papers there would be no such controversy!

The modern historian, who looks with some skepticism on the claims of art, music, literature, and philosophy as faithful indices of a national character, readily acknowledges the more sweeping claims of what it is fashionable to call cultural anthropology.

Indubitably the new United States lacked, and would lack for decades to come, a Culture of its own, but it did have a culture that was distinctive and perhaps even unique. In the formal arts Americans were, of course, imitative or, more simply, acquisitive, but not in those great common social denominators that suffused a sense of unity: equality and a classless society, with all the consequences that a Tocqueville would later trace from that seminal principle; schooling for most children, and popular enlightenment; the indulgence of children, and of women; the habit, almost the instinct, of private association for public purposes; voluntarism and pluralism in religion, and a common Protestant faith; self-government at the local levels; the assumptions of security, comfort, and well-being; the practices of husbandry and an intimate relation to the soil, to animals, to the weather; the habit of early marriage and of large families; social and physical mobility; stricter standards of morality, especially sexual morality, than obtained in the Old World; practical resourcefulness and inventiveness; mechanical and industrial proficiency; the assumption of even-handed justice in courts of law. A people, then, who had no formal Culture of their own boasted a cultural unity deeper and more pervasive than that which could be found in many of the nations of the Old World. This was the basis for that uniformity of habit, manners, dress, speech, work, play, politics, religion, and philosophy which was to impress every foreign visitor for a century. In America nationalism did not impose a pattern of society, but society imposed its pattern on nationalism.

*

Look, then, at some of the essential ingredients of nationalism which the new nation lacked, or had only in part: how did she provide them or make them superfluous? Clearly the first and most important was a national government. "A nation without a national government," said Alexander Hamilton, "is an awful spectacle," and he was right, as usual. The story of how Americans went about the task of providing themselves with a national government and its appropriate political machinery is both elaborate and familiar, yet we should not take it all for granted. It was not decreed by Nature, or the Genius of History, but something that had to be worked out. The Americans had enjoyed a common government in London for a century and a half, but it was neither of their making nor their choosing, nor was it sufficiently to their liking to excite imitation. In 1775 they were called upon to create a government *de novo*—something no numerous people had ever done before—and to do it under the stress of war, and in such a way as to satisfy the apprehensions of thirteen states which thought of themselves as independent and the expectations of a people who thought that government belonged to them.

The speedy creation of a national government was perhaps the most astonishing achievement of that generation of nation-makers, and the most enduring. It required a higher degree of political wisdom and resourcefulness than any people had heretofore displayed. This the Americans discovered. In a single generation they invented—it is possibly the most original invention in the history of democracy—the institution of the constitutional convention; drew up the first written Constitutions for State and Nation; created the first workable federal system in history and endowed it with power to grow and expand without serious difficulty by substituting the principle of the coordinate state for the practices of Old World colonialism; and fixed effective limits on governments thus created—separation of powers, checks and balances, bills of rights, and judicial review. Thus they solved, at one stroke as it were, those problems of government that had perplexed statesmen and philosophers since Pericles.

The ideas behind these solutions were not new; what was new was their institutionalization. What Americans did, in the words of John Adams, was to "realize the theories of the wisest writers." As James Wilson put it, with pardonable exaggeration, in the Pennsylvania ratifying Convention:

> The science of government itself seems yet to be almost in a state of infancy. Governments in general have been the result of force, of fraud and of accident. After a period of six thousand years has elapsed since the Creation, the United States exhibit to the world the first instance of . . . a nation, unattacked by external force, unconvulsed by domestic insurrections, assembling voluntarily, deliberating fully, and deciding calmly concerning the system of government under which they would wish that they and their posterity should live.

An intensely practical people, Americans provided a second, and essential, ingredient by contriving the political machinery required to implement their new institutions. Here, too, they revealed an inventiveness of the highest order, for their most important mechanisms were new. An elective President was a stroke of genius; never before had a large nation chosen the head of state by suffrage, direct or indirect. Providence made it both possible and popular by providing a Washington with all the Plutarchian virtues, and no vices, and, by processes unimagined at the time, the President became the focal point of popular nationalism. Providence intervened again by providing for a long succession of Presidents who had been Founding Fathers, and who had the glamour of the Argonauts. How astonishing that the men who wrote the Declaration of Independence presided over the destinies of the nation for another fifty years: never before, or since, has a nation been so fortunate.

A second political invention, a dual judiciary, was no less remarkable; it made possible the adjudication of all major prob-

lems, controversies, and quarrels in courts of law, and thus operated as a safety valve for the union, which worked until 1860.
Along with this went a subsidiary, but no less striking, invention:
judicial review, which substituted the magistracy of the law for
the coercion of the sword. A third invention, so prodigious that
it should rather be called a creation, was the political party. Most
British scholars delude themselves that the English invented the
political party, and Swedes, eager to claim some political contrivance before the welfare state, remind us somewhat plaintively of
the Hats and the Caps. But these—the Whigs and the Tories, the
King's Friends, the Bloomsbury Gang, the Hats and the Caps,
were not parties at all but precisely those factions and cliques
against which the Founding Fathers, and most famously Washington, so solemnly, so monotonously, and so rightly warned the
American people. The modern political party—the party that
grows from the people up, not the Crown down, the party that
eschews ideology and addresses itself to the task of winning office
and running the government, the party that is, above all, national, not regional, denominational, or personal—was an American invention, and it has some claim to be considered the most
successful of political inventions that made democracy work. It
took over the task of educating the people and thus helped create
a sophisticated electorate essential for self-government; it took
over the task of running politics and government and thus
welded together separated powers, and the disparate parts of a
federal union; it was a training school for practical democracy at
the grass-roots level; it made a permanent bureaucracy unacceptable; it was the most successful of nationalizing mechanisms.

Third, the Americans were required to find substitutes—or
compensations—for two of the most familiar of Old World national institutions: the Military—a term which embraces army
and navy, the officer elite, war, and a national enemy, with all
their affiliations, social, economic, and political—and the Church.

Though the new nation had been born out of war, united by war, and was personified in a military hero, its repudiation of the military was convulsive. Not only was the military rigorously subordinated to the civilian authority, it was all but eliminated: the military establishment of the United States stood at eighty in 1784, and was increased to 1,273 in 1790. And notwithstanding two wars with Britain and a quasi-war with France, within a single generation, American nationalism was not nourished on national antipathies. There were, briefly, such antipathies to Britain, but Britain was, after all, the mother country; for all her sins she escaped Jacobinism and Infidelity and much was therefore forgiven her; while the British themselves were no good at nursing grudges and in time apologized handsomely for fighting the Revolutionary War and completely forgot the War of 1812. Besides, American victories at Yorktown, on Lake Erie, and at New Orleans, where the Hunters of Kentucky destroyed the British Army with a loss of eight men (total British losses 2,036, total American 21), made it easy for Americans to forgive their quondam enemy.

There were no other national rivalries or antipathies of any importance in the nineteenth century. Canada never posed a serious threat, nor did Mexico; it was rather the other way around, and the United States played, unsuspectingly, the role of traditional enemy to Mexican and to Canadian nationalism. There were dangers from European powers, but these passed with the purchase of Louisiana, the Monroe Doctrine, and the annexation of Texas and Oregon; after 1815 geographical isolation and the deflection of European interests elsewhere gave the Americans a sense of security which few Old World nations could enjoy. The Monroe Doctrine did not meet a wall of resistance, but filled a void.

Providence and pride provided two convenient substitutes for a national enemy. The first was the Indians, who were, to earlier generations of Americans, what Germany was to the French, Russia to the Finns, Austria to Italians, and England to the Irish, though in each case the analogy is a bit out of kilter. For almost two hundred years Indians furnished a threat, and a focus for fear and for hatred, common to successive frontiers from the Bay Colony of the seventeenth century, and Georgia in the eighteenth, to the High Plains of the late nineteenth. The Indian was primitive, he was cruel, and he was there, and to kill him off and take his lands was not only a temptation but a contribution to Progress. What is more—and this was additional proof, if proof were needed, that Heaven was on the side of the Americans—in the long run he was sure to be defeated. Americans, therefore, almost alone of western nations, had the advantage of a common enemy who was sufficiently dangerous to induce common action, sufficiently romantic to inspire a vast popular literature, and sufficiently weak and backward to insure ultimate defeat. No other common enemy contributed so enduringly to nourish nationalism. All Americans could engage in Indian wars, at least imaginatively; all too could share in the romantic idealization of the Indian, once he was out of the way; two centuries after Pontiac's Conspiracy, a century after Custer's "Last Stand," American children still play at Indian and cowboy, and their parents watch westerns on film and television.

There was a second substitute for war, one that was achieved without danger, without cost, and almost without challenge. That was an abstraction called The Old World. The Old World was the enemy; it was the best of all enemies for it was a Moral Enemy, and to oppose it, therefore, was a sign of high-mindedness but cost nothing. Young Philip Freneau had struck this note as early as 1774:

> What are the arts that rise on Europe's plan
> But arts destructive to the bliss of man . . . ?

Blest in their distance from that bloody scene,
Why spread the sail to pass the Gulphs between?

Look to America, and what a contrast greets the eye:

Here Paradise anew shall flourish, by no second Adam lost
No dangerous tree or deathful fruit shall grow,
No tempting serpent to allure the soul
From native innocence. . . .

A quarter-century later President Jefferson could "bless the almighty being who, in gathering together the waters under the heavens in one place, divided the dry land of your [Old] hemisphere from the dry land of ours," and Hezekiah Niles could write of the War of 1812 that "dreadful as it is, [it] will not be without its benefits in separating us from the strumpet governments of Europe." It was the most persistent theme in American literature, but that was harmless enough; it was one of the persistent themes in American politics, which was not harmless.

Whatever the drawbacks of these substitutes—the destruction of the Indian, spiritual vanity and moral arrogance in Americans—they meant that in the United States nationalism could flourish without the glorification of the military, without standing armies or big navies or a military class. American literature has no military tradition; the only American battle songs come from the Civil War and are for the most part highly sentimental, and "God Save the Queen" is more belligerent than "My Country 'Tis of Thee." American painting is but little concerned with battles or warriors; American military law was long undeveloped and still is; West Point and Annapolis, for all their distinction, never had the social prestige of Sandhurst or Dartmouth, and are popularly admired, today, for their prowess in football. We have only to contemplate the part

188

contemplate the part played by national antipathies and by the military in the development of French, German, Italian, and Japanese nationalism in the nineteenth century, or their importance to the emergent nationalities of the Jewish and Arab states, or to China to appreciate how Providential the American experience has been; we have only to contemplate recent developments to suspect that Providence may have deserted us.

Americans repudiated the ecclesiastical Establishment as they repudiated the military, and proved that it was possible for nationalism to flourish without a national church. Europe could not imagine a State without a Church or, for that matter, a Church without a State, and France and Spain successfully imposed the connection upon their New World colonies, but not England. From the beginning American nationalism was both secular and tolerant. This meant, in turn, that American nationalism was never seriously threatened by religious disputes; that the United States escaped anything like the struggle over Catholic Emancipation, or the crisis of State-Church relationships in Italy which meant that the Vatican did not recognize the existence of Italy until 1929. It meant, too, that Americans could be conservative without being religious, and be radical without being irreligious! It did not mean that the United States was without a religion. Quite the contrary. For good measure the new nation began with two religions, one spiritual and one secular. Almost all Americans acknowledged themselves Christians—Justice Story, indeed, was prepared to prove in a court of law that the United States was a Christian nation—and if an earlier generation did not indulge in the antics of present-day Congressmen who want to come to the aid of God with a Constitutional Amendment, it was perhaps because they had no need to. For all the bewildering variety of denominations, Americans generally shared what has been called a "civic religion," a belief, in the words of Jefferson, in "an adoring and overruling Providence which by all its dispensations proves that it delights in the happiness of man here and his greater happiness hereafter." Along with this was a secular faith in America herself, in democracy, equality, and freedom which were equated with America, in the American mission and the American destiny.* America herself was a religion, and those who worshipped together at her altar shared a common religious experience.

There remained one major ingredient of nationalism—in the opinion of historians the most important of them all—a common past. "A nation," said Edmund Burke, "is a deliberate choice of ages and generations. . . . It is made by peculiar circumstances . . . which disclose themselves only in a long space of time." No wonder he missed the significance of the new American nation; it did not fit into his preconceptions, so it did not exist.

What was the United States to do? It had, as yet, no common history, no common body of memories, sacrifices, glories, afflictions, regrets; no usable past. Yet here, too, Americans displayed a resourcefulness, even a virtuosity, as unexpected as it was unprecedented. Phalanx after phalanx moved in and took over. They announced that they had no need of a past which was, after all, nothing but a melancholy record of folly and vice. They substituted the future for the past, a future shimmering with glory, and one which they could confidently preëmpt because they, and they alone, were untrammeled. Cooper's John Cadwal-

*Out of a hundred possible quotations we can select one from Jefferson and one from Tom Paine. "The preservation of the holy fire is confided to us by the world," wrote Jefferson to the Rev. Samuel Knox in 1810, "and the sparks which will emanate from it will ever serve to rekindle it in other quarters of the globe." And from *Common Sense:* "O ye that love mankind! Ye that dare oppose not only the tyranny but the tyrant, stand forth! Every spot of the old world is overrun with oppression. Freedom hath been hunted round the globe. . . . Europe regards her like a stranger and England hath given her warning to depart. O receive the fugitive and prepare in time an asylum for mankind."

lader put it well. "You complain," he said to his traveling companion, the bachelor Count,

> of the absence of association to give its secret, and perhaps greatest charm which such a sight [of the American West] is capable of inspiring. You complain unjustly. The moral feeling with which a man of sentiment and knowledge looks upon the plains of your [Eastern] Hemisphere is connected with his recollections; here it should be mingled with his hopes. . . . The speculator on moral things can enjoy a satisfaction here, that he who wanders over the plains of Greece will seek in vain . . . [for] here all that reason allows may be hoped for on behalf of man (*Notions of the Americans*).

Not content with the future, the Americans, with a kind of audacious intellectual imperialism, annexed the whole past of Europe and assimilated it to America. As we were the heirs not only of England but of the whole of Europe, so we could claim the whole European past: Homer and Virgil, Aquinas and Luther as well as Shakespeare and Milton. Yet this was a kind of rhetorical stop-gap; it carried conviction, but did not induce satisfaction. What Americans needed was a past of their own and once the need was clear it was supplied. In no time at all Americans equipped themselves not merely with history, but with legends, myths, memorials, shrines, symbols, heroes, and—with some difficulty—villains. Plymouth Rock was unfamiliar to the Pilgrim Fathers, but in 1820 the otherwise skeptical George Ticknor could write that "The Colosseum, the Alps, and Westminister Abbey have nothing more truly classical, to any one who feels as he ought to feel, than this rude and bare rock": Ticknor's observation was better as history than as architectural criticism. By 1820 then, the task of conjuring up a usable past was well under way.

The nation was fortunate in its Founding Fathers: what other nation had progenitors so authentic, so familiar, and so noble? Clearly Washington was marked out by Nature to be a hero, and soon Parson Weems helped Nature along. Noah Webster filled his *Spellers* and his *Readers* with patriotic anecdotes, and so too did the McGuffey brothers when their turn came. Stuart and Trumbull and Peale immortalized the Fathers on canvas; Alexander Wilson and Audubon captured the flora and the fauna of the New World in brilliant colors; and George Catlin caught the authentic Indian. None wrought more effectively than the poets and the storytellers, Irving, Cooper, and Hawthorne, and Longfellow, Whittier, and Lowell. None of this was too sophisticated for schoolchildren or too simple for their parents. Soon, too, the new nation was adequately provided with symbols: a flag designed by one of the Signers, and made by Betsy Ross and superior to any other flag because it taught easy lessons in geography; a Bell to ring out the gospel of Liberty; a popular song, "Yankee Doodle," and an elevated one, "Hail Columbia"; three Latin mottoes—*E Pluribus Unum, Annuit Coeptis,* and *Novus Ordo Saeclorum;* an eagle whose presence on the Great Seal somehow lifted that emblem into the empyrean; an Uncle Sam who could not only hold his own with John Bull but even look down on him; a Declaration of Independence and a Constitution whose preambles any schoolboy could learn, if he would.

One of the astonishing features of nation-making in America was its democratic character. Adam Smith had noted this in his *Wealth of Nations:* "The persons who now govern . . . their continental Congresses, feel in themselves at this moment a degree of importance which . . . the greatest subjects of Europe scarce feel. From shopkeepers, tradesmen and attorneys, they are become statesmen and legislators." Elsewhere nations had been made, and were to be made, by dynasties, armies, churches, and even intellectuals. In the United States the nation was a creation of the people themselves. Everybody participated—everybody who was white, anyway, and in a curious fashion even those who were not, for the Negroes gave to America much of its folklore, music, speech, gastronomy, and social and cultural habits. Immigrants contributed as well as native-born; women as well as men; the poor and the humble, because there were so many of them, as much as the rich and the distinguished. All participated in the colonization of successive wests; fought—and won high rank— in the miscellaneous armies; attended public schools; joined churches, political parties, labor unions, professional and fraternal organizations and even ran them. The contribution of the voluntary association to self-government is familiar; its contribution to national unity has been no less impressive.

In its democratic and equalitarian character, as in its lack of dependence on history, on the military, on national antipathies, and on the church, the emergence of American nationalism, then, is a striking departure from Old World norms. In another respect, too, the contrast dramatizes the divergent paths of Old and New World nationalism: the impact and the use of romanticism.

Almost everywhere in the Old World the emergency of modern nationalism was associated with romanticism; indeed from the literary and philosophical view nationalism itself can be regarded as a function of romanticism. The Age of Reason had been a cosmopolitan one that took dynastic struggles in its stride, and did not permit quarrels among monarchs to disturb the unity of the community of arts, letters, and science. It was, by its very nature, suspicious of everything merely local, parochial, traditional, and emotional, and thus suspicious of nationalism itself.

But romanticism smiled with approval upon nationalism, which did precisely associate itself with whatever was parochial, traditional, and emotional. And romanticism looked to the past —to some mythical golden day, or to the actual Middle Ages;

cherished origins, traditions, legends, the picturesque, the Gothic, and the sentimental. It addressed itself to recovering and exalting the past—folktales and folklore, poetry and ballads, the early laws and customs of society, the national language and even local dialects.

Romanticism was as pervasive in the New World as in the Old, and found comparable expression in literature, art, architecture, history, and sentiment. But though the expression was comparable it was not at all similar, except in the South which was the most European part of America and therefore the least distinctively American. As American romanticism could not look to the past, it looked to the future. As early as 1770 the Rev. Jacob Duché, later Chaplain to the Continental Congress, wrote, "I tread the hallowed soil of America with far higher pleasures from anticipation than your classic enthusiasts feel from reflection," and the contrast to the attitude of the classicists was equally valid for the attitude of the romanticists. It was no accident that so many European romantics looked to the New World for their Utopia; that the French should adore Franklin for his rustic simplicity rather than for his sagacity; that Chateaubriand should set his romance in the wilds of Florida; that Southey should idealize the Pennsylvania forests and be enraptured with the music of the word Susquehanna; that Coleridge should draw on America for inspiration for *Kubla Khan*, and that even so clear-headed a pair of observers as Tocqueville and Beaumont should immerse themselves in the romanticism of the American forest. And surely it is more than fortuitous that Audubon and Wilson, Bodmer and Miller and Bierstadt, who bathed the American wilderness in a sea of romanticism, should all be European.

In America the romantic could feed on reality, the real was romantic and the romantic was real. Americans naturalized romanticism, took it away from its sponsors and gave it back to the realists. We can see the curious blend in much of American

literature, in art, even in politics. We can see it most ostenta-
tiously in the treatment of the Indian and of Nature, a relatively
simple matter for Europeans but a very complicated one for
Americans, for Cooper, for example, or Washington Irving, or
William Gilmore Simms, even for later ethnologists like School-
craft and Morgan and Bandelier.

It was in part for this reason that American romanticism did
not, except in the South, associate itself with the past, with reaction, with religion, with the military, or with class consciousness.
Outside the South, Americans could indulge in romanticism
without succumbing to its logical consequences: they could be
romantic and democratic, equalitarian, secular, and progressive.
What James Madison wrote in the Federalist Papers was valid for
this, and for almost every, chapter of American experience:

> Is it not the glory of the people of America that while they
> have paid a decent respect to the opinions of former times and
> other nations, they have not suffered a blind veneration for
> antiquity, for custom, for names, to overrule the suggestions
> of their own good sense, the knowledge of their own situation,
> and the lessons of their own experience.

*

We can see now that the Fathers not only brought forth a new
nation but so conceived it and so dedicated it that it would long
endure. In the past 185 years nation after nation has come into
being, many of them made on what we may call the American
rather than the Old World model. How few of those made since
1789 have survived intact: Germany torn asunder; Italy racked by
civil war and dictatorship; the nations of Latin America swept by
revolution after revolution; Poland, Bohemia, Turkey, the Baltic
States conquered, overthrown, or dismembered beyond recognition. How few of the new nations that have come into being in

the last quarter century have escaped turbulence and revolution, how few show promise of survival. How astonishing then, in the light of history, that notwithstanding the Civil War, the United States should still have the same Constitution, the same Bill of Rights, the same—or almost the same—federal union, the same republican and democratic systems, the same rule of law, the same legislative and executive bodies, even the same political parties, that were set up at the beginning. How astonishing that the ingredients of nationalism so deliberately assembled and combined in that first quarter century proved so harmonious and so enduring.